CW01590274

All About Dinosaurs

A children's reference guide to everything you wanted to know about dinosaurs!

Illustrated by:
Norma Burgin, Mark Dolby, Graham Kennedy,
Peter Komarnysky, Damian Quayle, Neil Reed,
Pete Roberts (Allied Artists), James Field, Terry Riley (SGA),
Mike Atkinson, Chris Forsey, Rob Shone, Q2A Media

Design by Design Principals, Warminster, UK

This edition published by Parragon in 2012

Parragon
Queen Street House
4 Queen Street
Bath BA1 1HE, UK
www.parragon.com

ISBN 978-1-78186-078-6

Printed in China

iknow stuff

All About Dinosaurs

A children's reference guide to everything you wanted to know about dinosaurs!

Parragon

Bath • New York • Singapore • Hong Kong • Cologne • Delhi
Melbourne • Amsterdam • Johannesburg • Shenzhen

Contents

Introduction

The dinosaurs lived on Earth from about 250 million to 65 million years ago. They were found all over the world, in deserts and forests and grasslands. Their relatives lived in the air and in the water.

This book tells you about the different types of dinosaurs. In the final chapter you can also learn about their world and why they eventually became extinct. Look in this chapter to find out what words like 'Jurassic Period' mean.

At the back of the book is a list of useful words, and an alphabetical index of the creatures included.

Ancestors of the dinosaurs

Life first appeared on Earth about 3.5 billion years ago. The first simple life-forms lived in the sea. From there, life gradually moved onto the land and into the sky. One group of animals that became very successful in prehistoric times was the reptiles.

What are reptiles?

A reptile is a vertebrate animal. That means it has a backbone, like mammals and birds. Today, most reptiles live on land, but crocodiles live on land and in water, and turtles and some snakes live in water.

Reptile characteristics

A reptile is cold-blooded and has scaly skin. It lays eggs with hard shells.

When reptiles ruled the Earth

Millions of years ago reptiles were the most successful animals on the Earth – just like mammals are today. The reptiles' rule lasted from about 250 million years ago to 65 million years ago.

Baryonyx was a large fish-eating dinosaur.

DID YOU KNOW?

There are nearly 6,000 species of reptiles still living in the world today.

Modern reptiles

Lots of reptiles, such as dinosaurs, died out (became extinct) 65 million years ago. But others, including crocodiles, lizards, turtles and snakes, lived on.

Prehistoric reptiles

Dinosaurs ruled life on land for nearly 200 million years. Meanwhile, pterosaurs filled the skies and plesiosaurs swam in the sea.

Diplodocus was a sauropod – a giant plant-eating dinosaur.

Brachiosaurus was one of the biggest sauropods.

The origin of reptiles

The first reptiles developed from another group of animals called amphibians, which had adapted to life on land. Amphibians were the first creatures to have legs and feet instead of fins.

Feet versus fins

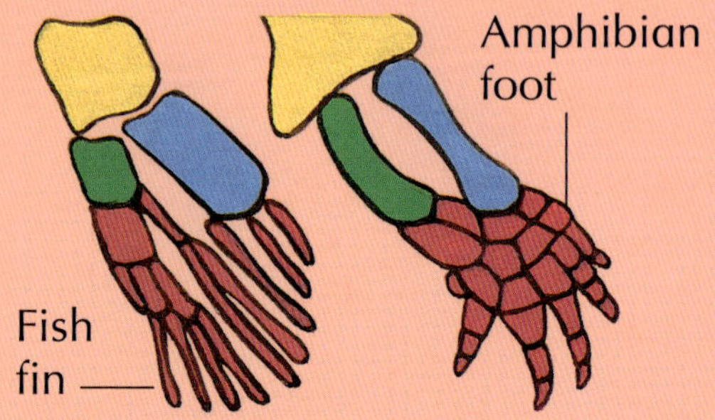

An amphibian's foot is different from a fish's fin. It has fingers and toes, which allow it to walk, climb and dig on land.

Living a double life

Amphibians are able to walk on land and swim in the water. Just like frogs and newts now, the first amphibians had to lay their soft, jelly-covered eggs in water. The eggs would have dried out if laid on land.

Leaving the water

Early amphibians started to spend more time on dry land to avoid being gobbled up by hunters, such as fish and water scorpions.

Living on dry land

As the early amphibians spent more and more time on dry land, they gradually changed. Their smooth skin became covered in scales. And they began to lay eggs with hard shells on land. They became the world's first reptiles.

Modern amphibians

There are more than 4,200 different species of amphibians alive today. These are divided into three groups. Frogs and toads are in one group, newts and salamanders in another, with worm-like creatures called caecilians in the third.

Acanthostega

This amphibian was one of the first land animals that had four legs, and feet with toes. Like other amphibians, *Acanthostega* evolved from fish that had fleshy, bony fins.

Fish-like but four legs

Acanthostega had a tail like a fish and gills for breathing in water. But it had the legs and feet of a land animal.

Happiest in the water

Its weak legs show that *Acanthostega* was probably more at home in the water than on land. It could swim well, using its legs as paddles. But it could also have dragged itself around on the shore as it hunted for food to eat.

DID YOU KNOW?

The world's biggest amphibian today is the Chinese giant salamander, which can grow up to 1.5 metres long.

Varied foods

Acanthostega could snap up fish in water. It also caught insects and other small creatures on land.

Acanthostega's feet

This amphibian had webbed feet, just like ducks and geese today. Its feet would have helped it push its way through the water. Each foot had eight toes.

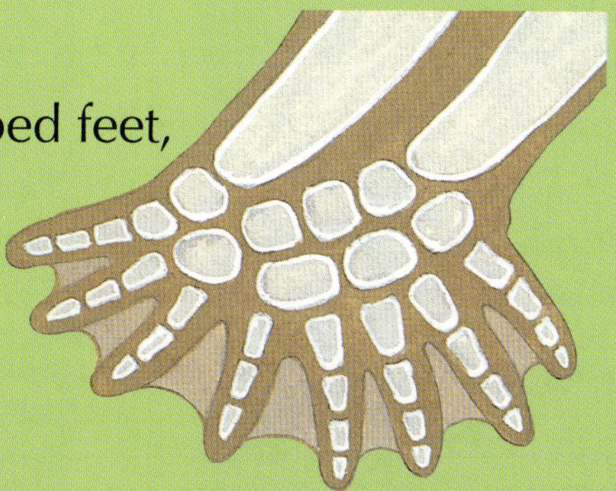

Acanthostega hunting insects on land.

Acanthostega facts

Lived: 370 million years ago

Found: Greenland

Length: 60 centimetres

The first reptiles 1

The world's first reptiles appeared between 350 and 300 million years ago. They had legs instead of paddle-like limbs, and they laid eggs with hard shells.

Petrolacosaurus

This slender lizard-like reptile was probably a fast-moving hunter. Like lizards today, it raced around, snapping up insects to eat.

Petrolacosaurus facts

Lived: 300 million years ago

Found: North America

Length: 40 centimetres

Westlothiana

Some experts think that this creature was more like an amphibian than a true reptile. *Westlothiana* lived close to water and caught creatures such as spiders and insects.

Westlothiana facts

Lived: 350 million years ago

Found: Europe

Length: 30 centimetres

Reptile eggs

Reptile eggs have a hard shell which keeps the contents from drying out. This means that reptiles can lay their eggs on land, not in water like amphibians have to.

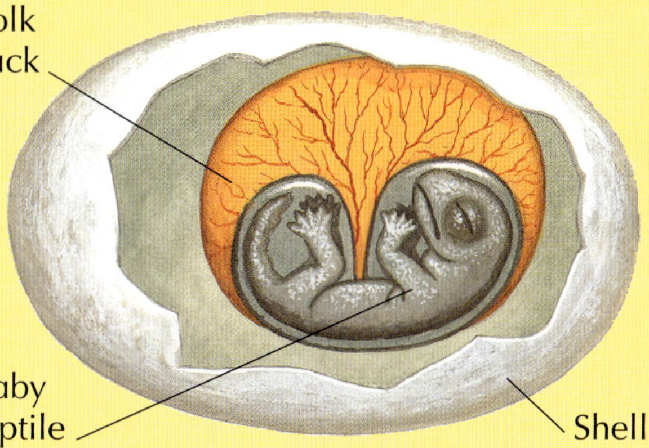

Paleothyris

Small, lizard-like *Paleothyris* hunted insects and other small creatures in its forest home. It had sharp teeth for seizing and biting its prey.

Paleothyris facts

Lived: 300 million years ago

Found: North America

Length: 30 centimetres

Pareiasaurus

It might look fierce, but this big, chunky animal ate only plants. Its skin was covered with lots of hard bony scales. These could have protected it from enemies and strengthened its heavy body.

Pareiasaurus facts

Lived: 250 million years ago

Found: South Africa, Europe

Length: 2.5 metres

The first reptiles 2

Among the early reptiles there were animals with lots of different features. Some of these survived while others did not. *Lagosuchus*, with its long legs, looks rather like the later dinosaurs, but was not a dinosaur.

Milleretta

This fast-moving little reptile probably fed on insects. There was a slight dip at the back of its head which may show it had ear drums. This would have meant it had good hearing that helped it find prey.

Scutosaurus

Heavy-bodied *Scutosaurus* ate the water plants that floated on lakes and pools. Its teeth had jagged edges which could easily cut through this tough food. Lots of bony knobs covered its skin and may have protected it from meat-eating hunters.

Milleretta facts

Lived: 250 million years ago

Found: South Africa

Length: 60 centimetres

Scutosaurus facts

Lived: 250 million years ago

Found: Europe

Length: 2.5 metres

Heavy legs and feet show this was a slow mover.

Lagosuchus

The shape of this reptile's body and its long legs show that it was a good runner, like many kinds of dinosaur. It could probably run fast to catch insects to eat, and to escape from predators.

Lagosuchus facts

Lived: 230 million years ago

Found: South America

Length: 40 centimetres

Reptile and amphibian hands

The shape of an animal's hand tells us something about its life. Amphibians' hands cannot hold things well, but can paddle in water. Reptiles have hands with long slender fingers – just right for seizing prey and for digging nests in the ground.

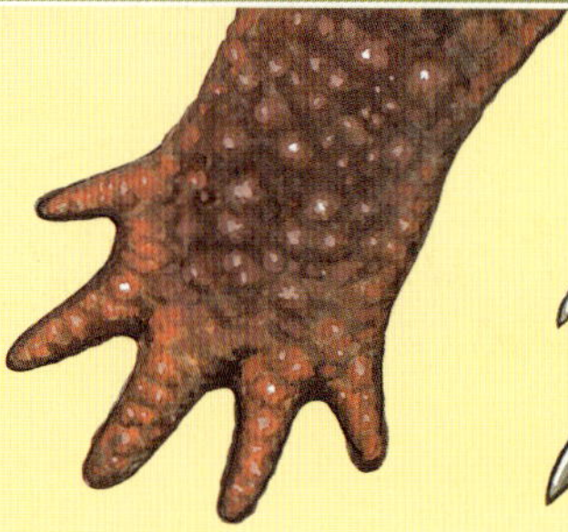

Amphibian hand

Reptile hand

The first reptiles 3

Some of the early reptiles had features similar to those of the dinosaurs that came later. Like dinosaurs, some had 'diapsid' skulls, which means that their skulls had two holes on either side.

DID YOU KNOW? When these reptiles were alive, most of the world's land was joined in one supercontinent called Pangaea. The word means 'all earth'.

Longisquama

This strange creature had two rows of long scales along its back. Some experts think it might have held these out at its sides to use like wings. But others believe they were brightly coloured and used to attract mates.

Longisquama facts

Lived: 230 million years ago

Found: Asia

Length: 15 centimetres

Paradapedon

This pig-like animal walked on all fours and fed on tough plants. It chomped through its food with the help of the strong beak at the front of its jaws.

Paradapedon facts

Lived: 210 million years ago

Found: Asia

Length: 1.3 metres

Ferns

Ferns grew on Earth long before flowering plants. They have large divided leaves called fronds and were an important food for creatures such as *Paradapedon*.

Holes in the head

There are three kinds of reptile. An anapsid has a box-like skull with no holes. Synapsids have one hole each side, and diapsids two holes. Muscles were attached across the holes, so jaws could be opened wider.

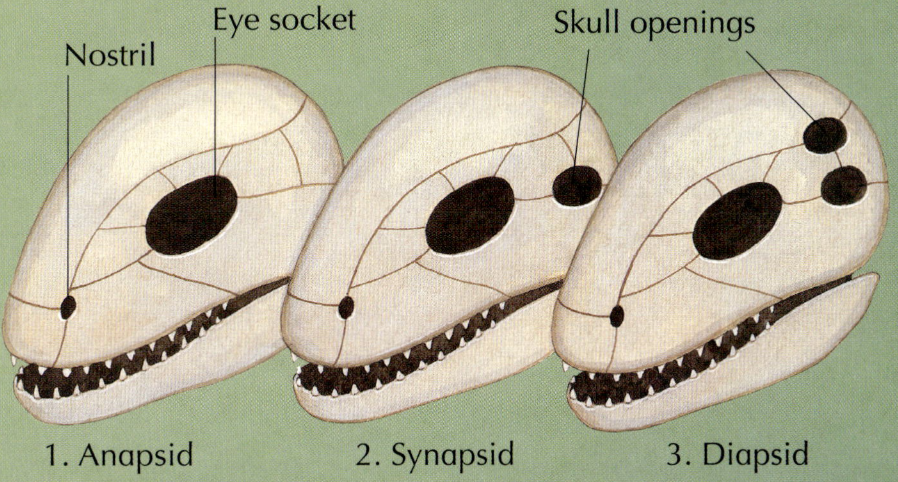

Hylonomus

Hylonomus was one of the very first reptiles discovered. Fossils were found in Nova Scotia, Canada in 1851. The reptile's name means 'forest mouse' and it lived on forest floors.

Lizard-like

Hylonomus looked like a small lizard and probably lived like one. Its body was long and slender and it had lots of small, sharp teeth. It was an anapsid reptile so it had a solid skull.

Hylonomus probably scurried around the forest floor.

DID YOU KNOW?

A fossil is part of an animal or plant that has turned into rock over thousands of years.

Hylonomus facts

Lived: 310 million years ago

Found: Canada

Length: 20 centimetres

Forest floor

Hylonomus lived among seed ferns and tree stumps on the forest floor. Here they searched for food and raised their young.

Sharp teeth

Hylonomus hunted for its food. It probably ate insects and other small creatures such as worms. Its sharp pointed teeth could cut through flesh and possibly even through hard snail shells.

Trapped inside tree stumps

A number of *Hylonomus* fossils were found together. The reptiles had probably climbed into a rotting tree stump to find food. They became trapped there and their remains were fossilized.

Pelycosaurs and mammal-like reptiles

About 80 million years before the first dinosaurs, two groups of reptiles appeared on the Earth. First came the 'sail backs', or pelycosaurs, from which evolved the mammal-like reptiles.

Edaphosaurus

This reptile had an amazing row of skin-covered spines on its back that looked like a large sail. It had lots of blunt teeth, shaped like little pegs. These were better suited to eating plants than meat.

Edaphosaurus facts

Lived: 280 million years ago

Found: N. America, Europe

Length: 3.5 metres

Dimetrodon

Fierce *Dimetrodon* was a predator. It had a big head and powerful jaws, packed with sharp teeth. Experts don't know what the huge 'sail' on its back was for, but it might have helped it keep warm or attract mates.

Dimetrodon facts

Lived: 280 million years ago

Found: North America

Length: 3.5 metres

Dimetrodon teeth

This reptile's name means 'two types of teeth'. It had long sharp teeth at the front of its jaws. Behind these were smaller teeth that would have been good for cutting through meat.

Moschops

Biggest of all the mammal-like reptiles was *Moschops*, which had a barrel-like body and thick legs. It fed on plants that it bit off using strong blunt teeth.

Moschops facts

Lived: 260 million years ago

Found: South Africa

Length: 5 metres

Mammal-like reptiles 1

The first mammal-like reptiles lived about 300 million years ago. They died out about 180 million years ago. These animals had skulls like mammals, but most walked like reptiles, with their legs out at the sides.

Horned head

Estemmenosuchus gets its name, which means 'crowned crocodile', from the horns on its head.

Estemmenosuchus

This big reptile lived around pools and lakes. It probably moved around in herds and ate both plants and animals. It may have used its horns in fierce battles with rival males, just like stags do today.

Estemmenosuchus facts

Lived: 255 million years ago

Found: Europe

Length: 3 metres

Thick bones may have protected the head in battles.

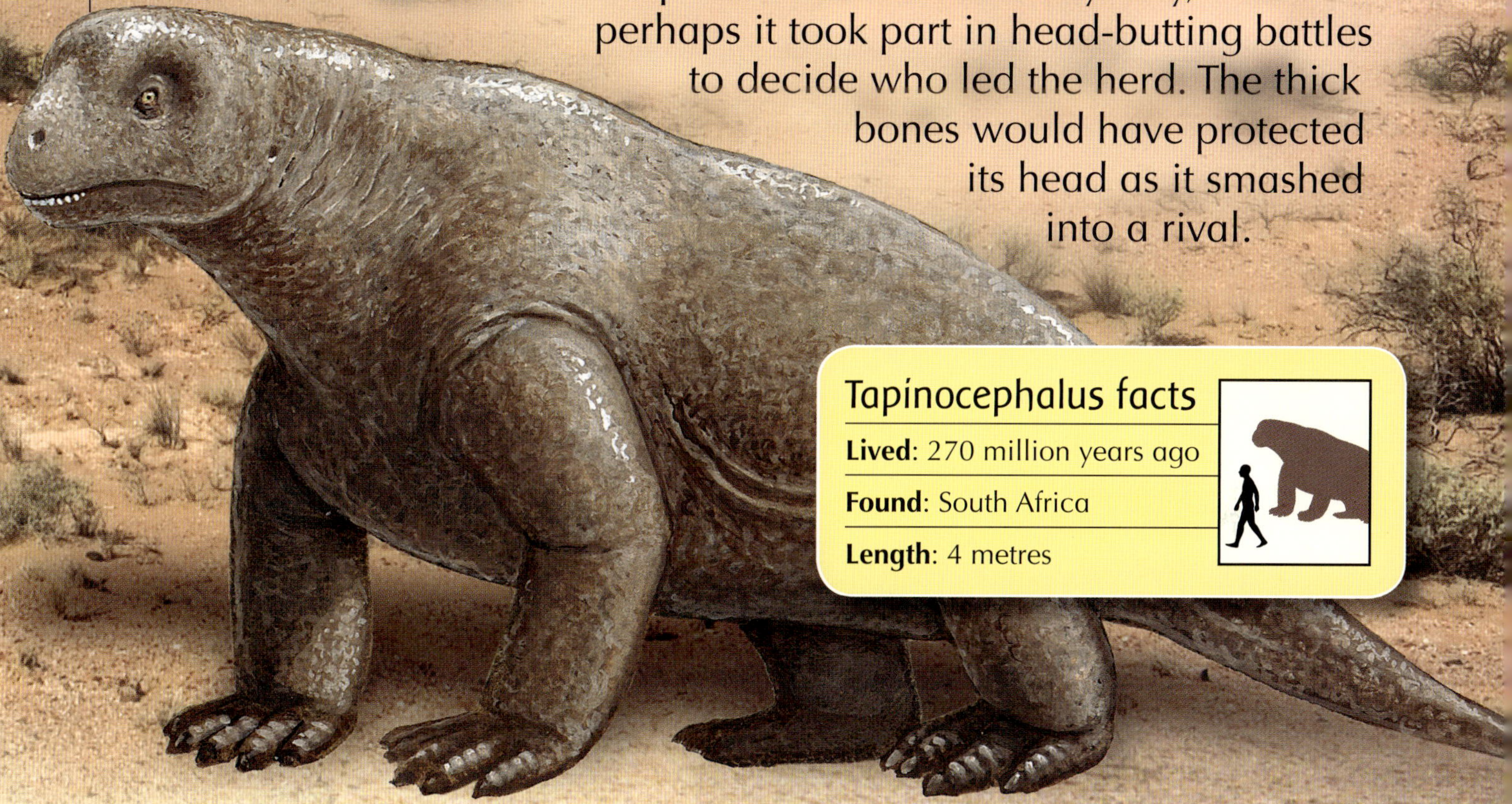

Tapinocephalus

This slow-moving plant-eater had a very thick skull. Experts don't know exactly why, but perhaps it took part in head-butting battles to decide who led the herd. The thick bones would have protected its head as it smashed into a rival.

Tapinocephalus facts

Lived: 270 million years ago

Found: South Africa

Length: 4 metres

Procynosuchus facts

Lived: 260 million years ago

Found: South Africa, Europe

Length: 60 centimetres

Procynosuchus

Meat-eating *Procynosuchus* belonged to a group of mammal-like reptiles called cynodonts. It could swim by wriggling its body and paddling with its webbed hands and feet.

Mammal-like reptiles 2

Later mammal-like reptiles were more like today's mammals. *Thrinaxodon*, for instance, may have had hair. And *Lycaenops* walked upright like a mammal, not with legs sprawled out at its sides like a lizard.

Lycaenops

This creature's name means 'wolf face' and it did look very like a wolf. It had strong jaws and big pointed teeth for tearing prey apart.

Lycaenops facts

Lived: 260 million years ago

Found: South Africa

Length: 1 metre

Plants as food

At the time of the mammal-like reptiles there were no flowering plants or grasses like those we know today. But there were plenty of plants for the reptiles to eat, such as tree ferns, conifers and horsetails.

DID YOU KNOW?

Mammal-like reptiles dominated life on Earth for 80 million years. Mammals, like us, are descended from these reptile ancestors.

Thrinaxodon

Thrinaxodon looked very like a mammal. It could breathe while eating – something mammals can do but most reptiles can't.

Thrinaxodon facts
Lived: 250 million years ago
Found: S. Africa, Antarctica
Length: 50 centimetres

Lystrosaurus

This mammal-like reptile lived rather like a hippo today. It probably waded into lakes and fed on plants that it cropped with the bony beak at the front of its jaws.

Lystrosaurus facts
Lived: 250 million years ago
Found: S. Africa, Asia, Antarctica
Length: 1 metre

The Permian mass extinction

About 252 million years ago, at the end of the period of time known as the Permian, something terrible happened on the Earth. Huge numbers of animals on land and in the sea were wiped out for ever. No one knows exactly what caused this, but there are lots of different ideas.

Death from volcanoes

Many volcanoes erupted at this time. The eruptions sent carbon dioxide and other gases into the air. These may have created acid rain that killed plants. Animals would have starved to death.

Death by suffocation

Lots of volcanic eruptions meant there would have been more of the gas called carbon dioxide in the air. Animals would have found it hard to breathe and may have suffocated.

Death from space

Another possibility is that a space rock called a meteorite hit the Earth at this time. The impact of the rock could have made volcanoes erupt, filling the air with poisonous gases and killing plants and animals.

Death by freezing

Some experts think that it became very, very cold on the Earth at the end of the Permian. Ice spread from the North and South Poles. Perhaps the weather was so cold for such a long time that lots of animals died.

Once plants and plant-eaters died, it would have become harder and harder for the meat-eaters to find food.

Pangaea

As land masses moved to form the huge supercontinent called Pangaea, sea levels changed. This might have made life difficult for sea creatures living in shallow waters, but doesn't explain why so many land animals died.

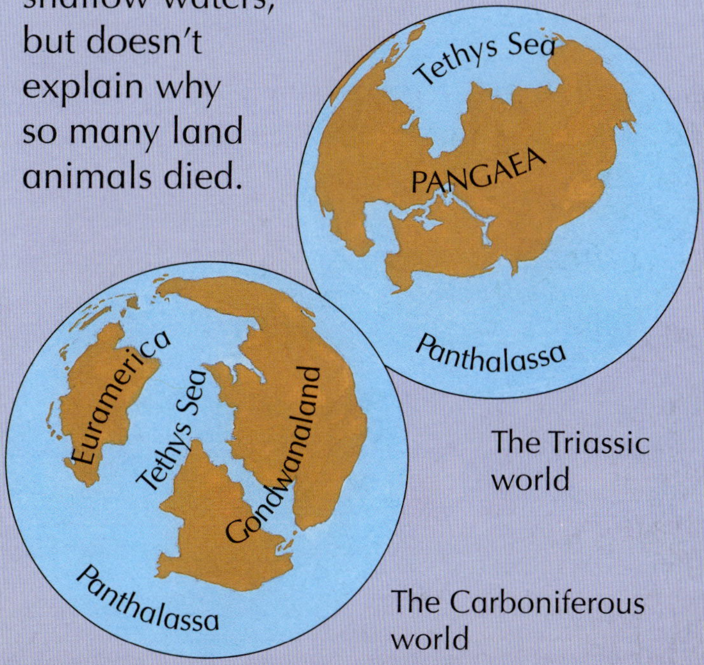

The Triassic world

The Carboniferous world

Mammal-like reptiles 3

Lots of mammal-like reptiles were wiped out in the mass extinction 248 million years ago. But some, such as *Cynognathus*, survived and they were the ancestors of mammals today.

Cynognathus

This fierce creature probably hunted in packs and attacked much larger animals such as *Kannemeyeria*. It may have had a hairy coat.

This reptile's name means 'dog jaw'.

Cynognathus facts

Lived: 230 million years ago

Found: South Africa, South America, Antarctica

Length: 1 metre

Kannemeyeria

Kannemeyria's only teeth were the two tusks growing from its top jaws. It didn't have any other teeth, but it could bite off mouthfuls of plant food with its strong beak.

Placerias

A plant-eating reptile, *Placerias* may have used its big tusks to dig up roots and other food. It could cut through the toughest plants with its sharp beak.

Placerias facts

Lived: 215 million years ago

Found: North America

Length: 3.5 metres

Teeth like a mammal's

Cynognathus had several sorts of teeth. At the front were sharp teeth for attacking prey and it also had long fang-like canine teeth. Further back were cheek teeth with sharp points for cutting through flesh.

Kannemeyeria facts

Lived: 230 million years ago

Found: South Africa, Asia, South America, Antarctica

Length: 3 metres

Killers and scavengers

The first meat-eating dinosaurs appeared about 225 million years ago. They included the world's biggest-ever predators. These killers terrorized the world's plant-eaters for more than 160 million years, until all the dinosaurs died out 65 million years ago.

Theropods – the meat-eaters

All meat-eating dinosaurs are called theropods. The name means beast feet. Most of these dinosaurs moved upright on their slender back legs. They could run fast – much faster than the plant-eaters they hunted.

Creature features

Most of the meat-eating dinosaurs had bird-like feet with clawed toes. They had sharp-clawed hands for attacking and holding onto their prey.

Hand and foot of a meat-eating dinosaur.

Changes over time

Meat-eating dinosaurs adapted over millions of years. Later species were more intelligent and had longer legs and sharper eyes than earlier predators.

DID YOU KNOW?

A *Tyrannosaurus's* back feet were as long as 1 metre.

Teeth and beaks

Many of the meat-eaters had strong jaws and big teeth. Others had toothless beaks which they might have used for cracking eggs.

The first meat-eaters

These dinosaurs first appeared about 225 million years ago, during the Triassic. They were smaller than later predators like *Tyrannosaurus*, and not such fierce hunters.

Coelophysis

This dinosaur was built for speed. Its leg bones were almost hollow which made it light and able to run fast.

Coelophysis facts

Lived: 220 million years ago

Found: North America

Length: 3 metres

Eoraptor

One of the earliest dinosaurs, *Eoraptor* moved quickly on its slender back legs. It was a meat-eater, but it may have also eaten animals that were already dead. This is called scavenging.

Eoraptor's long jaws were lined with lots of small saw-edged teeth.

Eoraptor facts

Lived: 225 million years ago

Found: South America

Length: 1 metre

Herrerasaurus

Another fast-moving hunter, *Herrerasaurus* had arms that were much shorter than its legs. It held its tail straight out behind it when it ran to balance its weight.

Herrerasaurus facts
Lived: 220 million years ago
Found: South America
Length: 3 metres

Fast movers

Meat-eaters had to be sure-footed as well as fast, so they could turn at speed when chasing prey and still keep their balance.

Going fishing

Some of these small predators, such as *Eoraptor*, may have fed on fish as well as hunting land animals.

Giants 1

Later species of meat-eating dinosaurs were much bigger than the earliest types. These huge creatures had strong teeth for biting meat and sharp claws for tearing at their prey's skin.

Dilophosaurus

This dinosaur probably moved in groups, searching for prey. The crest on its head may have been brightly coloured and used to attract mates or to signal to others in its group.

Allosaurus

The largest meat-eater of its time, *Allosaurus* was a huge creature with big powerful back legs and a thick S-shaped neck. Its teeth had jagged edges for slicing through flesh.

Dilophosaurus facts

Lived: 190 million years ago

Found: North America

Length: 6 metres

Scavengers

Meat-eating dinosaurs may have been scavengers as well as hunters. This means they ate animals that had died of old age or disease, or had been killed by others. By scavenging, an animal gets a meal without much effort.

Allosaurus facts

Lived: 140 million years ago

Found: North America

Length: 12 metres

Giganotosaurus

This massive hunter was even larger than *Tyrannosaurus*. Its biggest teeth were an amazing 20 centimetres long and could slice deep into the flesh of its prey.

Giganotosaurus facts

Lived: 90 million years ago

Found: South America

Length: 15 metres

Giants 2

Powerful bodies and razor-sharp teeth and claws made these dinosaurs very good hunters.

Ceratosaurus

This dinosaur had a large head, with a short horn on the tip of its nose and big horny bumps near its eyes. It might have showed these off to help attract mates in the breeding season.

Ceratosaurus facts
Lived: 150 million years ago
Found: North America, Africa
Length: 6 metres

Pack hunters

Meat-eating dinosaurs probably hunted in packs. Together, they could attack and kill animals much larger than themselves – even giant sauropods.

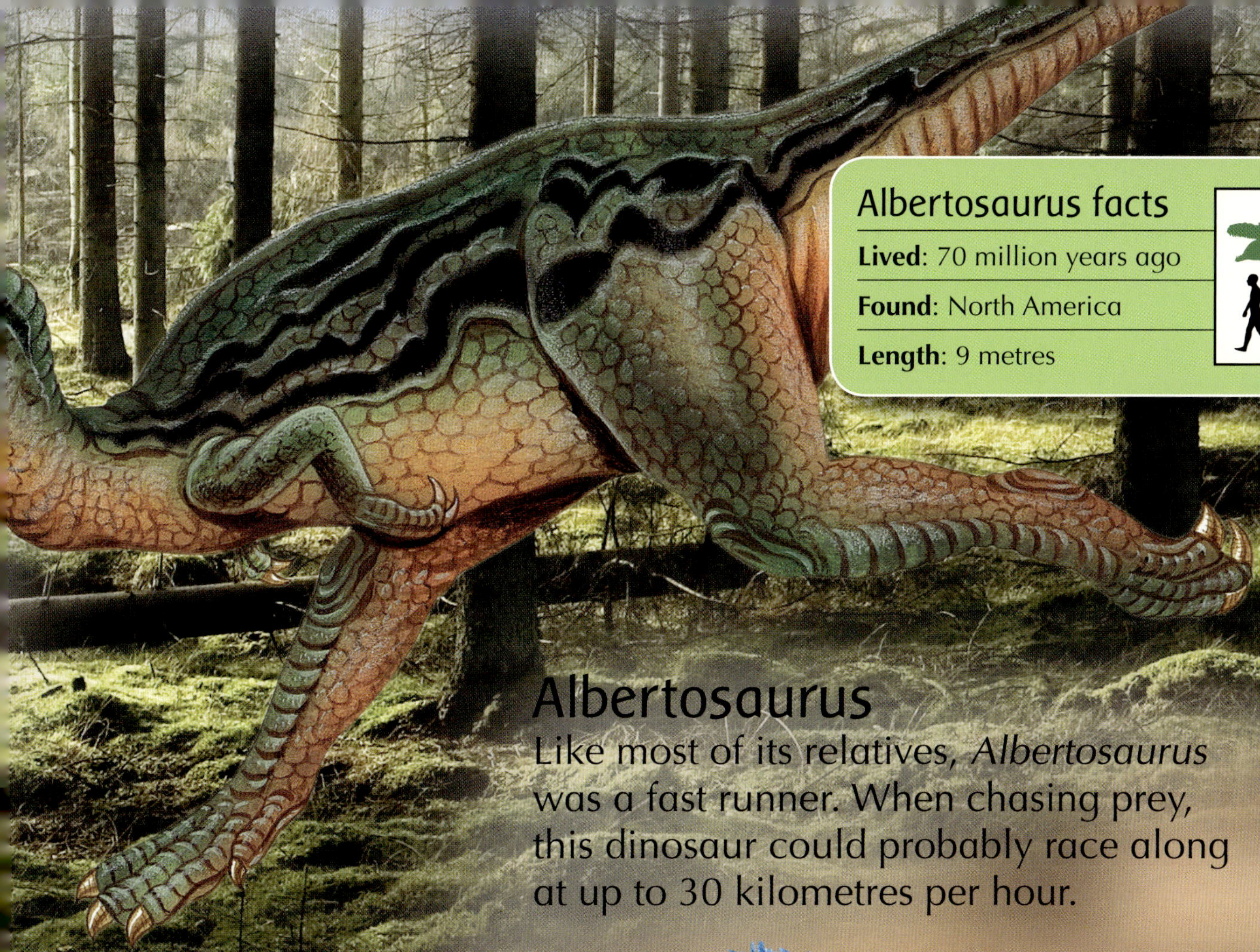

Albertosaurus facts

Lived: 70 million years ago

Found: North America

Length: 9 metres

Albertosaurus

Like most of its relatives, *Albertosaurus* was a fast runner. When chasing prey, this dinosaur could probably race along at up to 30 kilometres per hour.

There was a hard beak at the end of the jaws.

Therizinosaurus

This dinosaur had claws up to 70 centimetres long. It may have used them to break open termite nests or to cram plants into its mouth.

Therizinosaurus facts

Lived: 70 million years ago

Found: Asia

Length: 12 metres

Spinosaurs

The spinosaurs' huge sails were made of long spines covered with skin. The sail may have helped the dinosaur control its body temperature, or been used to attract mates or frighten off enemies.

Soaking up the sun

A spinosaur might have sat with its sail in the sun each morning, soaking up enough heat to keep it warm and active all day long.

Spinosaurus

Like other spinosaurs, this huge dinosaur fed on fish that it caught in its long, toothy jaws.

The sail may have been brightly coloured.

Spinosaurus facts

Lived: 100 million years ago

Found: Africa

Length: 15 metres

Baryonyx

Baryonyx walked upright on its back legs. Its head was narrow and it had a long nose, like a crocodile. Most big meat-eating dinosaurs had S-shaped necks, but *Baryonyx*'s neck was straight. Its tail was long and heavy.

Baryonyx facts

Lived: 125 million years ago

Found: Europe

Length: 10 metres

Irritator facts

Lived: 100 million years ago

Found: South America

Length: 8 metres

Irritator

Irritator had crocodile-like jaws packed with hook-shaped teeth for snaring fish.

Ornithomimids

These dinosaurs looked a lot like the big flightless birds, such as ostriches, that we know today. They ran upright on their long back legs and had toothless beaks.

Deinocheirus

Only the arm bones of this dinosaur have ever been found, but experts think it was an ornithomimid.

Gallimimus

When *Gallimimus* ran, it held its long tail straight out behind it to help it keep its balance. This was one of the largest of the ornithomimid dinosaurs.

DID YOU KNOW?

Deinocheirus had enormous claws that were up to 25 centimetres long.

Gallimimus facts

Lived: 70 million years ago

Found: Asia

Length: 6 metres

Deinocheirus may have been twice the size of *Gallimimus*.

Deinocheirus facts
Lived: 70 million years ago
Found: Asia
Length: Uncertain

A mixed diet

Ornithomimids probably ate plants as well as small creatures. Their long fingers and sharp claws were the right shape for digging for insects and plants.

Long, slim legs show that this dinosaur was a fast mover.

Ornithomimus

Like all ornithomimids, this dinosaur could run fast to catch prey and to escape from danger.

Ornithomimus facts
Lived: 70 million years ago
Found: North America
Length: 3.5 metres

Dromaeosaurs

All these dinosaurs were very fierce hunters. They had big sharp claws on their feet and strong hands for grabbing hold of their prey.

Utahraptor

The claw on *Utahraptor's* second toe was 38 centimetres long. The dinosaur attacked prey with these killer claws while holding on tightly with its strong hands.

Utahraptor facts

Lived: 125 million years ago

Found: North America

Length: 6.5 metres

Dromaeosaurus

This dinosaur, like other dromaeosaurs, could speed along at 60 kilometres per hour. It had lots of sharp teeth and a large curved claw on each foot.

Dromaeosaurus facts

Lived: 70 million years ago

Found: North America

Length: 1.8 metres

Clever hunters

Dromaeosaurs probably hunted in packs, working together to bring down much larger animals.

Oviraptor

This meat-eating dinosaur lived in desert areas in Asia. It probably moved and hunted in groups. Unlike most dinosaurs, *Oviraptor* took good care of its eggs and may also have looked after its young once they hatched.

Oviraptor facts

Lived: 80 million years ago

Found: Asia

Length: 1.8 metres

'Dino-birds'

These small meat-eating dinosaurs looked like birds, with feathery arms and big beaks. They could even use their clawed feet to climb into trees.

Archaeopteryx

Archaeopteryx had feathers like a bird, but teeth and a bony tail like a reptile. It may have been able to fly short distances.

Archaeopteryx facts
Lived: 150 million years ago
Found: Europe
Length: 60 centimetres

Taking to the trees

Like birds, feathered dinosaurs could dart about in trees to find food and escape from enemies.

Protarchaeopteryx

Its feathery arms and tail make this dinosaur look a lot like a bird, but it probably couldn't fly.

Protarchaeopteryx facts

Lived: 150 million years ago

Found: Asia

Length: 1 metre

DID YOU KNOW?

Bambiraptor was named after Bambi because of its small size.

Bambiraptor

This little dinosaur was about the size of a chicken and had a covering of downy feathers. It couldn't fly, but it could run fast to catch prey such as small reptiles and mammals.

Bambiraptor facts

Lived: 75 million years ago

Found: North America

Length: 1 metre

Deinonychus

Deinonychus hunted in packs. This meant that it could attack and kill prey that was much larger than itself.

A pack of *Deinonychus* attacking a large plant-eating dinosaur.

Dinosaur fact

Deinonychus facts

Lived: 110 million years ago

Found: North America

Length: 3 metres

This meat-eater was a fierce hunter that had deadly claws on each foot.

Claws

Deinonychus means terrible claw. It got this name because of the curved claw on the second toe of each foot, which could grow up to 13 centimetres long.

Speedy hunter

Deinonychus ran fast on its long back legs, holding its tail out behind to help it balance. On its hands were three fingers, each with a sharp curved claw.

Killers or scavengers?

Deinonychus was one of the top hunters of its time and area. But it may have eaten animals that were already dead as well as hunting for its own prey.

Tearing teeth

Deinonychus's jaws were packed with lots of teeth with jagged edges. Some were up to 8 centimetres long.

Dinosaur fact

Velociraptor facts

Lived: 70 million years ago

Found: Asia

Length: 1.8 metres

The name *Velociraptor* means speedy thief.

Feathered beast

In 2007, a fossil of *Velociraptor* was found to have bumps on its arms like feathered birds today. This dinosaur was probably too big to fly, but its feathers may have been used to help cover its nest and eggs.

Fierce killer

Velociraptor was a fast-moving hunter. It had sharp, serrated teeth and a large sickle-shaped claw on each foot. It held the largest foot claws off the ground when it wasn't attacking prey. This meant that the claws didn't get worn down and blunt.

Velociraptor

Velociraptor may have hunted in packs, but scientists do not have enough evidence to be sure of this.

Tail rudder

This probably helped it balance and gave stability when turning, especially at high speeds.

Locked in battle

One *Velociraptor* fossil was found locked in battle with a *Protoceratops*, a medium-sized plant-eater.

Intelligent hunter

Velociraptor had a large brain in relation to the size of its body and its intelligence was the highest of all the dinosaurs. This would have helped make it a very effective hunter.

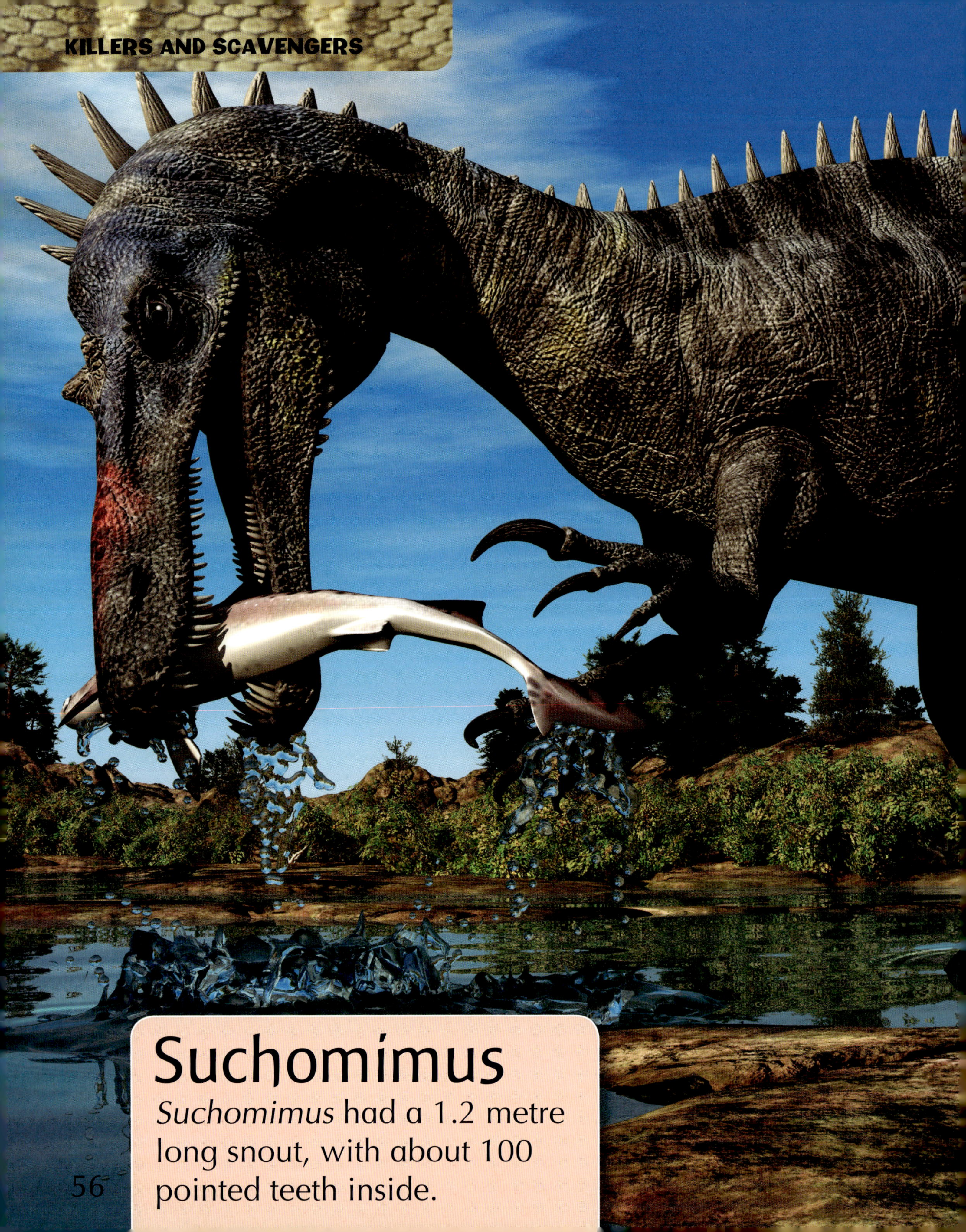

Suchomimus

Suchomimus had a 1.2 metre long snout, with about 100 pointed teeth inside.

Suchomimus means crocodile mimic.

In 1997, scientists discovered about two-thirds of a skeleton of *Suchomimus*, the only one discovered so far.

Young bones

The *Suchomimus* skeleton belonged to a young animal, whose body was about 10.6 metres long, but scientists believe that adults may have grown to as much as 12 metres long.

Giant thumb claw

This dinosaur had three fingers on each hand. All the fingers were tipped with sharp claws, and the claw on each inside finger was extra long, perfect for spearing or hooking fish from the water.

Fishy diet

Scientists think that *Suchomimus* ate fish. Its arms were longer than those of other dinosaurs, and would have been good for dipping into the water to catch fish.

Swamp to desert

The area where the *Suchomimus fossil* was found is now desert, but when this dinosaur was alive, it was a wet, swampy place.

Dinosaur fact

Suchomimus facts

Lived: 105 million years ago

Found: North Africa

Length: 11 metres

Dinosaur fact

Tyrannosaurus facts

Lived: 70 million years ago

Found: North America

Length: 12 metres

Tyrannosaurus

Tyrannosaurus got as close as it could to its prey, before making a final high-speed dash and pouncing on it.

Tyrannosaurus bursts through the trees to attack its prey.

This mighty hunter lived towards the end of the dinosaurs' rule on the Earth.

Big head, big teeth

Tyrannosaurus had a huge head, up to 1.5 metres long. Its jaws were packed with 50 or 60 razor-sharp teeth. Some were 23 centimetres long – as big as a banana!

Small arms

This dinosaur's arms were so tiny they didn't even reach up to its mouth. But its claws were very useful for seizing hold of prey.

Powerful killer

Tyrannosaurus was strongly built and walked upright on its two big back legs. It held its tail out behind it to help balance the weight of its heavy head and chest. It had good eyesight for spotting its prey from a distance.

Full to bursting

Like lions and tigers today, *Tyrannosaurus* probably didn't eat every day. If it killed a large plant-eater it would gobble up as much as it could and be satisfied for several days.

Giant plant-eating dinosaurs

Biggest of all the plant-eating dinosaurs were the sauropods. Experts think these huge, long-necked dinosaurs were the largest animals ever to have lived on land.

The sauropods

The first sauropods lived about 220 million years ago and there were many different kinds. The name means 'lizard feet'.

Creature features

Sauropods walked on all fours on their big heavy legs. They all had long necks and tails, but their heads were very small.

Strong legs

A sauropod needed strong legs to support its heavy body. The biggest bones in a sauropod's body were its leg bones.

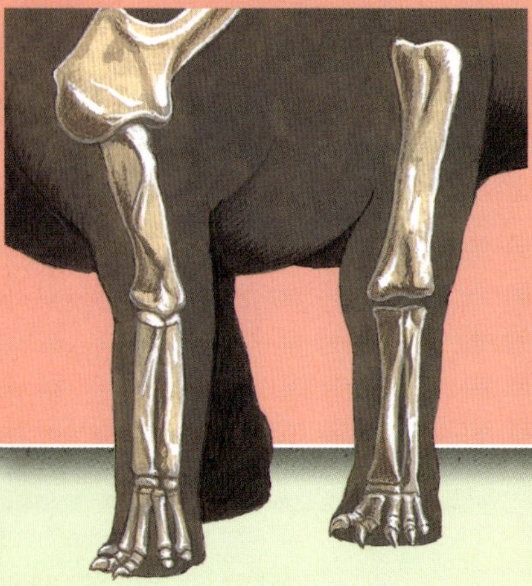

Food for all

Full-grown sauropods could feed on leaves at the tops of trees. Their young ate the leaves lower down.

Gulping their food down

Sauropods used their teeth for stripping leaves from branches. They couldn't chew properly so just gulped their food down whole.

A herd of *Diplodocus* feeds alongside other sauropods on the riverbank.

Camarasaurus

Big for defence

Being big helped protect sauropods from fierce predators. They couldn't run away quickly, but they could lash out at enemies with their long tails.

Where in the world?

Fossils of these dinosaurs have been discovered in most parts of the world, but none has been found in Antarctica yet.

Prosauropods

These dinosaurs lived before the sauropods, but they died out about 180 million years ago. Like the sauropods, they had long necks and small heads.

Riojasaurus facts

Lived: 220 million years ago

Found: South America

Length: 11 metres

Plateosaurus

Plateosaurus probably spent most of its time on all fours. But it may also have been able to rear up on its back legs to reach leaves high in the trees.

Plateosaurus facts

Lived: 220 million years ago

Found: Europe

Length: 7 metres

Riojasaurus

This was one of the largest of the sauropods. But it wasn't very heavy because some of its bones were hollow. This helped to keep its weight down.

Mussaurus

A full-grown *Mussaurus* was about the size of a hippo. It probably moved around in herds, looking for plants to eat.

Mussaurus facts

Lived: 215 million years ago

Found: South America

Length: 3 metres

DID YOU KNOW?

Mighty *Mussaurus* laid eggs that were only 2.5 centimetres long. That's smaller than a chicken's egg.

Massospondylus

Massospondylus was a typical prosauropod. It had a bulky body, a long neck and tail, and a small head. It lived in the early Jurassic period, before the huge sauropods.

Reaching up

This big plant-eater could probably stand up on its back legs for a short while to feed on leaves high in the trees.

Teeth like pegs

The peg-like teeth of this dinosaur were just the right shape for stripping leaves from branches.

Stomach stones

Some dinosaurs, such as *Massospondylus*, couldn't chew very well. Instead they swallowed stones that helped grind up the food into a mush in their stomach.

Tree-eater

The main foods of *Massospondylus* were the needle-like leaves of conifer trees, as well as gingko leaves and horsetail plants.

Thumb claws

This dinosaur had four sharp-clawed fingers on each hand. It also had an extra-large claw on each of its thumbs.

Massospondylus reaches up to eat some gingko leaves.

Massospondylus facts

Lived: 200 million years ago

Found: Africa, North America

Length: 5 metres

Cetiosaurs

These were some of the earliest sauropods. All had a heavy body and a solid backbone. Some later sauropods had bones that were partly hollow, which made them lighter.

Cetiosaurus

Cetiosaurus is famous for being the first sauropod to be discovered. Its giant bones were found in England in 1809.

Barapasaurus

Barapasaurus had a long tail and neck like other cetiosaurs. Its spoon-shaped teeth had jagged edges for stripping leaves from branches.

Barapasaurus facts

Lived: 200 million years ago

Found: Asia

Length: 18 metres

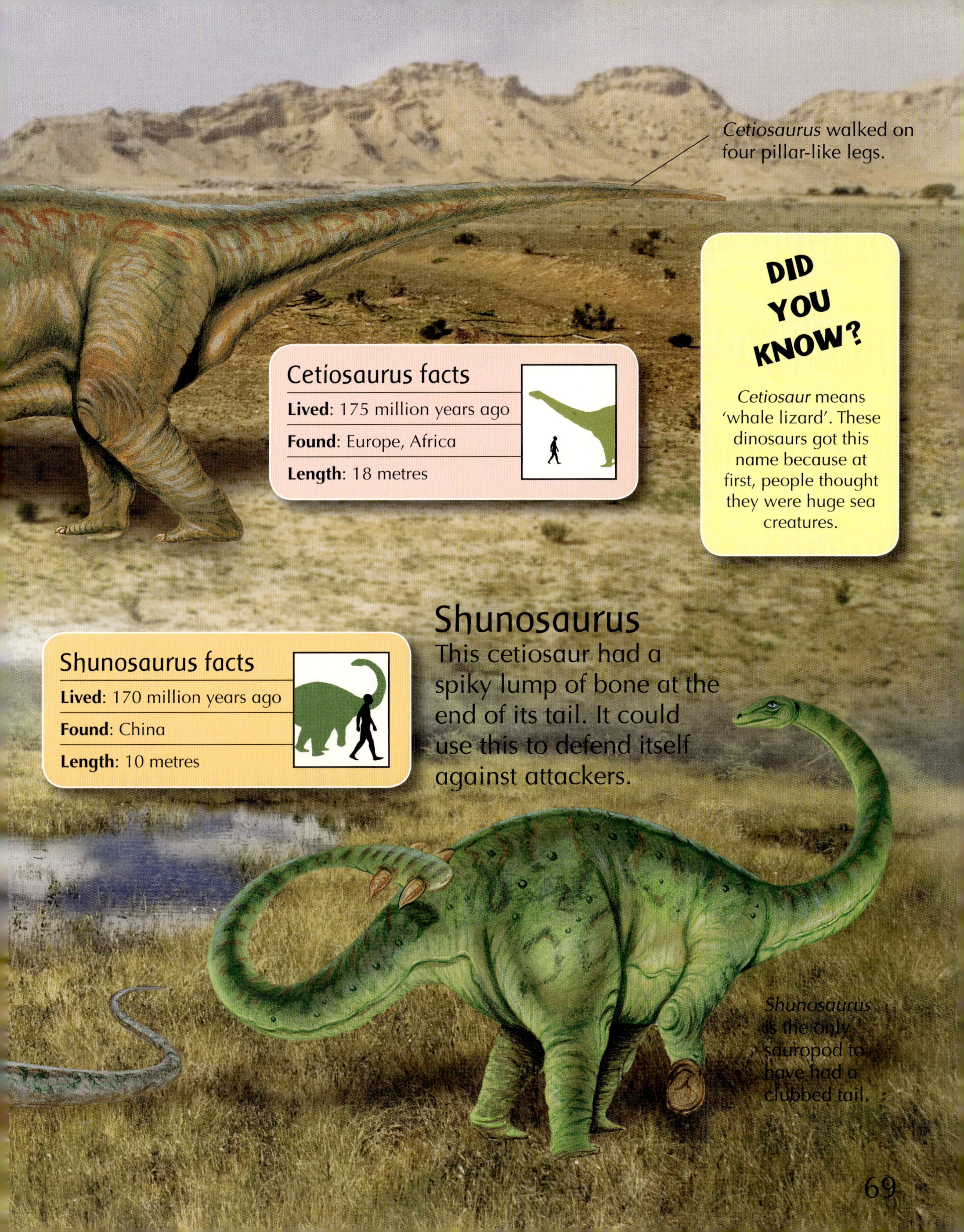

Cetiosaurus walked on four pillar-like legs.

Cetiosaurus facts

Lived: 175 million years ago

Found: Europe, Africa

Length: 18 metres

DID YOU KNOW?

Cetiosaur means 'whale lizard'. These dinosaurs got this name because at first, people thought they were huge sea creatures.

Shunosaurus

This cetiosaur had a spiky lump of bone at the end of its tail. It could use this to defend itself against attackers.

Shunosaurus facts

Lived: 170 million years ago

Found: China

Length: 10 metres

Shunosaurus is the only sauropod to have had a clubbed tail.

Camarasaurs

These sauropods first lived in the late Jurassic period. Unlike other giant plant-eaters, camarasaurs had teeth that pointed forwards.

Twigs

Camarasaurus was able to feed on the hard parts of plants because of its strong teeth.

Camarasaurus's teeth were more than 4 centimetres wide.

Camarasaurus

This dinosaur's strong jaws were packed with big spoon-shaped teeth. They were shaped for cutting through twigs and branches.

Camarasaurus facts

Lived: 150 million years ago

Found: N. America, Europe

Length: 18 metres

Euhelopus facts

Lived: 150 million years ago

Found: Asia

Length: 15 metres

Euhelopus

Many sauropods had teeth only at the front of their mouth. *Euhelopus* had teeth all round its jaws, as did *Camarasaurus.*

DID YOU KNOW?

Euhelopus's neck was an amazing 5 metres long and was made up of 19 vertebrae. Even a giraffe has only 7 vertebrae in its neck.

Camarasaurus skull

Its skull shows that this dinosaur had big eyes and nostrils. It probably had good senses of sight and smell.

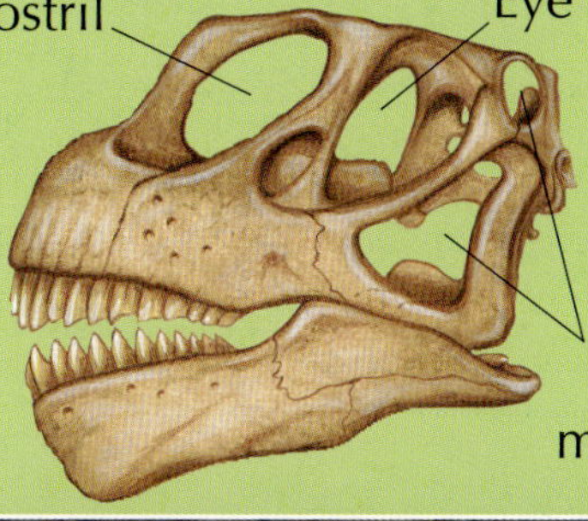

Diplodocids 1

This group of dinosaurs includes the longest animals that have ever lived on the Earth. There were lots of these dinosaurs in the late Jurassic period.

Tail like a whip

A diplodocid's tail had a long, thin tip like a whip. The dinosaur could lash out against an attacker with its tail. This could cause serious wounds and scare the enemy away.

Mamenchisaurus's neck contained as many as 19 vertebrae.

Mamenchisaurus

This Chinese dinosaur had one of the longest necks of any dinosaur. It made up more than half the animal's length and it measured an amazing 14 metres long.

Mamenchisaurus facts

Lived: 160 million years ago

Found: Asia

Length: 25 metres

Seismosaurus

This was one of the biggest of the diplodocids. Only one skeleton has ever been found.

Seismosaurus facts

Lived: 150 million years ago	
Found: North America	
Length: 40 metres	

Barosaurus

Even though it was so huge, *Barosaurus* might have been able to rear up on its back legs to feed on leaves high in the trees. The dinosaur's big tail helped to support its weight.

Barosaurus facts

Lived: 150 million years ago	
Found: N. America, Africa	
Length: 27 metres	

DID YOU KNOW?

A diplodocid dinosaur could weigh over 30 tonnes, more than the weight of five full-grown elephants.

Diplodocids 2

Big dinosaurs like diplodocids may have lived to be more than 100 years old. During its life, a diplodocid would have eaten many tonnes of plant leaves, stems and twigs.

A neck frill?

The neck frill may have helped the dinosaur attract a mate. Or it may have been used to scare enemies away.

Supersaurus

This super-sized dinosaur was almost as long as two tennis courts. It may have weighed over 50 tonnes. These dinosaurs moved around in herds, feeding on plants.

Supersaurus facts

Supersaurus facts
Lived: 150 million years ago
Found: North America
Length: 42 metres

Amargasaurus

This dinosaur had a double row of spines on its back. These may have been covered with skin.

Amargasaurus facts

Lived: 130 million years ago

Found: South America

Length: 10 metres

Supersaurus had big broad feet to help support its great weight.

Small heads

Diplodocus was more than three times the size of meat-eating *Allosaurus*, but it had a smaller head.

Diplodocus

Experts used to think *Diplodocus* dragged its tail on the ground. But fossilized tracks show that it held its tail up as it walked.

Diplodocus is one of the biggest and best known of the diplodocids.

Although *Diplodocus* was long, it weighed only about 10 tonnes. This was less than some other sauropods.

Extra bones

There was an extra bone beneath each of the vertebrae making up this dinosaur's backbone. These extra bones strengthened the tail.

Diplodocus teeth

Diplodocus had 50-60 weak teeth in the front of its mouth, but no back teeth for chewing food.

Dinosaur fact

Diplodocus facts

Lived: 150 million years ago

Found: North America

Length: 27 metres

Fern-eater

Diplodocus probably couldn't lift its head very high. So it may have eaten lots of low-growing plants, such as ferns.

Long neck, tiny head

This giant dinosaur's neck could grow up to 8 metres long. But its head was tiny. It measured only about 50 centimetres.

Titanosaurs 1

This group of sauropods first lived in the late Jurassic. Their name means 'gigantic lizards'.

Argentinosaurus facts

Lived: 90 million years ago

Found: South America

Length: 30 metres

Alamosaurus

So far, *Alamosaurus* is the only titanosaur from North America. It lived until the end of the Cretaceous period, 65 million years ago, when dinosaurs were wiped out.

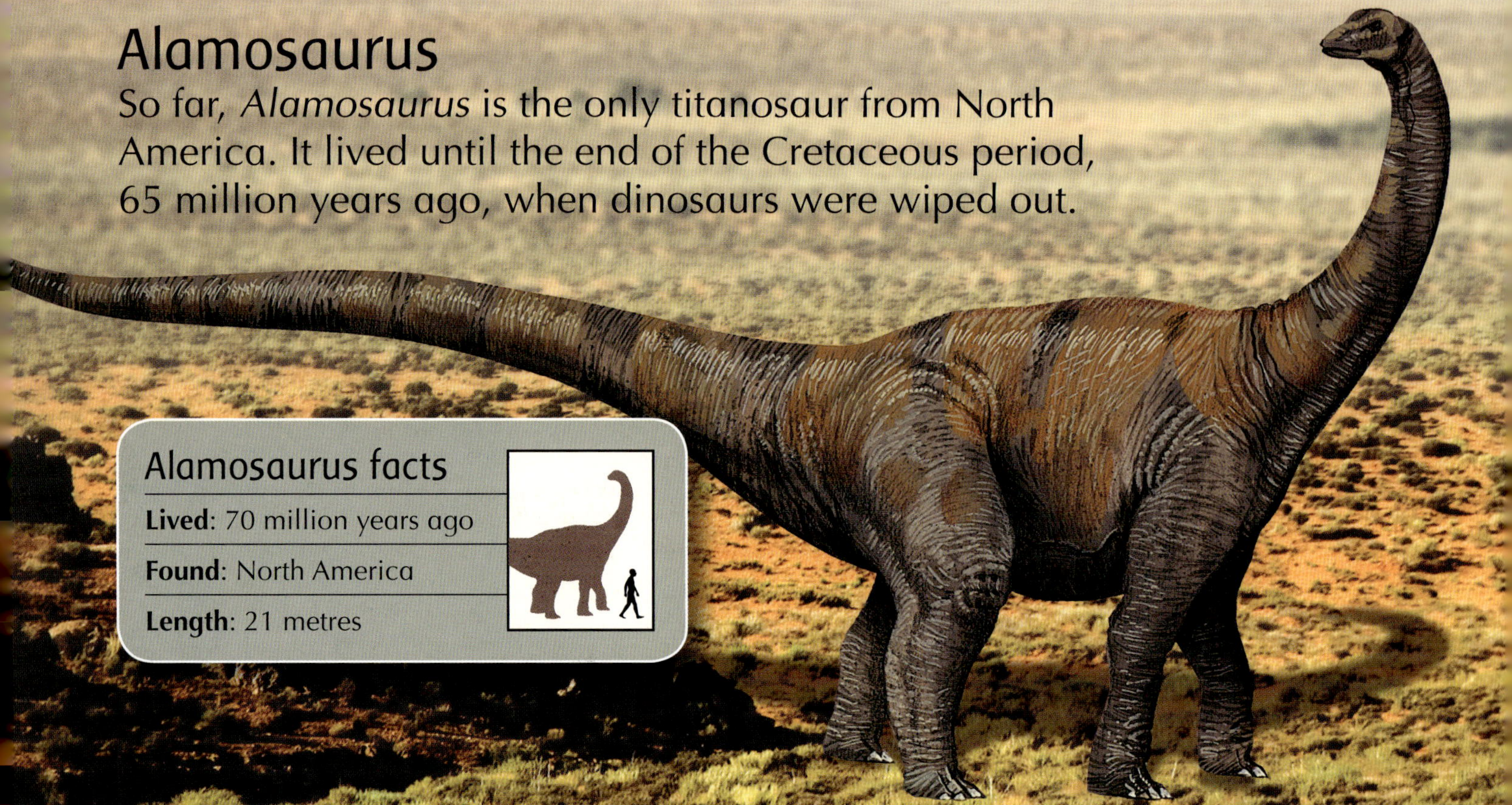

Alamosaurus facts

Lived: 70 million years ago

Found: North America

Length: 21 metres

Argentinosaurus

This enormous creature may have weighed as much as 100 tonnes. Only the biggest meat-eaters, such as *Giganotosaurus*, would have dared attack such a monster.

Body armour

Saltasaurus's back was studded with bony plates, about 10 centimetres across, and pea-sized lumps of bone.

Saltasaurus

Saltasaurus had a long neck and tail like other sauropods. But, unusually, it also had armoured skin that may have helped protect it from meat-eaters.

Saltasaurus facts

Lived: 80 million years ago

Found: South America

Length: 12 metres

Titanosaurs 2

Fossils of titanosaurs have been found in most parts of the world, but not in Australia or Antarctica. Some fossilized titanosaur eggs have been found in South America.

Paralititan

Like other titanosaurs, *Paralititan* had teeth like little pegs at the front of its jaws. It used these to strip leaves from branches.

Janenschia

Only one incomplete fossil of *Janenschia* has ever been found. Some experts think that it may belong to the camarasaur group of dinosaurs.

DID YOU KNOW?

Paralititan was one of the heaviest of all dinosaurs. It may have weighed 50–80 tonnes.

Janenschia facts

Lived: 155 million years ago

Found: Africa

Length: 24 metres

Paralititan facts

Lived: 95 million years ago

Found: Africa

Length: 25 metres

Where Paralititan lived

Paralititan lived in Africa, near the coast and in swamps where there were lots of plants to eat.

Strong heart

A sauropod dinosaur needed a big, strong heart to pump blood around its body. The heart had to work extra hard to pump blood right up to the sauropod's head.

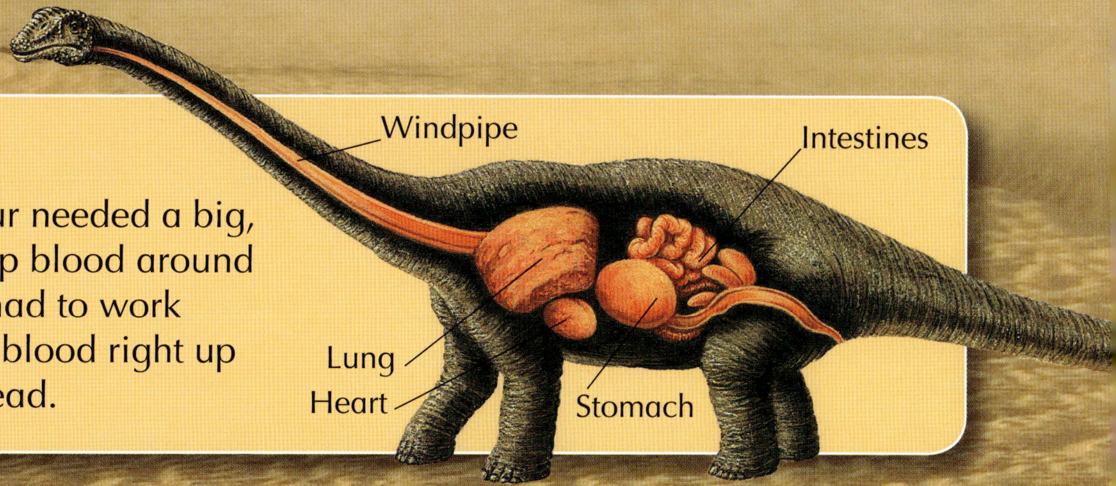

Dinosaur fact

Titanosaurus facts

Lived: 70 million years ago

Found: Africa, Asia, Europe, South America

Length: 20 metres

A herd of *Titanosaurus* dinosaurs arrives at the riverbank to drink.

Titanosaurus

Titanosaurus was a giant plant-eater. It swallowed stones to help grind down the food in its stomach.

Titanosaurus was named after the Titans in ancient Greek stories. The Titans had great strength.

Giant attackers

Big meat-eaters usually attacked the younger or weaker members of a *Titanosaurus* herd.

First fossils

The first fossil of this dinosaur to be found was a leg bone discovered in India in 1871. Soon more bones were dug up and scientists realized this was a new species of dinosaur.

Old and young

Titanosauruses lived together in a herd. This was a group of dinosaurs, old and young, that moved around together. Young animals walked in the centre of the herd for safety.

Plant-eaters

Flowering plants related to the magnolia had started to grow on Earth by *Titanosaurus's* time. The dinosaur fed on the leaves of these trees and others.

Dinosaur fact

Brachiosaurus facts

Lived: 150 million years ago

Found: Africa, Europe, N. America

Length: 25 metres

Brachiosaurus

Brachiosaurus needed lots of food. It may have eaten 200 kg of plants every day.

Brachiosaurus dinosaurs would have stripped the leaves from trees.

Brachiosaurus had big nostrils on top of its head. It may have been able to smell food before it could see it.

High and low

Brachiosaurus may have reared up on its back legs to reach high leaves. Or it may have kept all four feet firmly on the ground as it swung its long neck from side to side to find food.

Huge

Brachiosaurus had an amazingly long neck. This meant it could reach out and munch on lots of different plants without moving far.

Miniature brain

This huge creature had a small head for its body and a tiny brain. Its front legs were longer than its back legs, so its body sloped down towards its short tail.

Living in a group

Brachiosaurus probably moved around in a group, or herd. The dinosaurs would have spent most of their time looking for food and eating.

Armour, horns and plates

Sauropods were not the only plant-eating dinosaurs. Other kinds included armoured dinosaurs, stegosaurs and horned dinosaurs. They were all smaller than sauropods, but they had their own built-in body armour.

Plated, armoured, bone-headed and horned dinosaurs

All these groups of dinosaurs had horns or other bony lumps and bumps on their body. These helped protect them from meat-eaters.

Spiky tail

Stegosaurs had long, sharp spikes at the end of their tails.

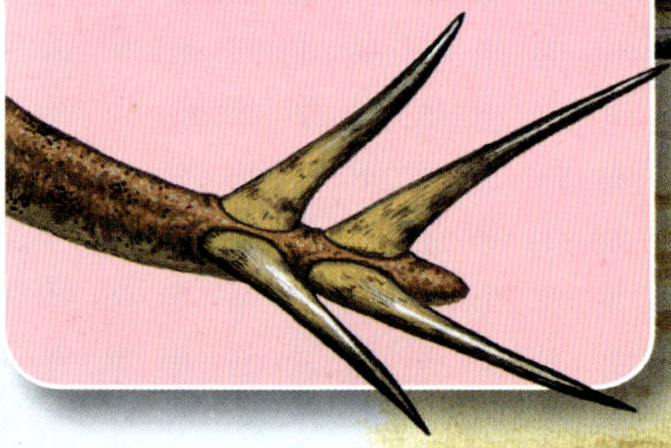

Plated dinosaurs

The plated dinosaurs were called stegosaurs. All had rows of large bony plates sticking up along the back.

Armoured dinosaurs

This group included nodosaurs and ankylosaurs. Both types had bony plates in the skin and spikes on the body.

Bone-headed and horned dinosaurs

These dinosaurs get their name from their heads, which had sharp horns or specially thickened bones.

DID YOU KNOW?

One of the biggest of the armoured dinosaurs was *Ankylosaurus*, which weighed around 4 tonnes.

Elephant-like legs

Most of these dinosaurs had thick legs, like those of an elephant. These legs were quite short and stiff but strong enough to carry the dinosaur's heavy body.

The nodosaurs

The first armoured dinosaurs were the nodosaurs. They all had lumps of bone set into the skin on their backs. This made them much harder for meat-eating dinosaurs to attack.

Minmi

Minmi was the first armoured dinosaur to be found in the southern hemisphere.

Unusually, bony plates also protected *Minmi's* belly.

Gastonia

This dinosaur was a fearsome sight. It had big sharp spikes sticking out of its sides as well as bony studs on its back.

Gastonia facts
Lived: 125 million years ago
Found: North America
Length: 2.5 metres

The spikes were up to 30 centimetres long.

Minmi facts

Lived: 115 million years ago

Found: Australia

Length: 3 metres

Dinosaur body armour

The skin of armoured dinosaurs was covered with pieces of bone. Some were flat, others pointed. In between were little bony lumps, about the size of a pea.

Edmontonia facts

Lived: 70 million years ago

Found: North America

Length: 7 metres

Edmontonia

Huge spines grew from the shoulders and sides of this dinosaur. They faced forwards and probably protected it from predators.

The ankylosaurs

These armoured dinosaurs had a special weapon. An ankylosaur had a lump of bone like a club at the end of its tail. It could swing this against an attacker.

Ankylosaurus

This dinosaur was one of the largest ankylosaurs. It had a big, rounded body, shaped like a barrel and was twice as wide as it was tall. Its legs were short but strong.

DID YOU KNOW?

An ankylosaur could break a tyrannosaur's leg with a blow from its clubbed tail.

Talarurus

Large bony spikes covered the back and tail of this ankylosaur. Like other ankylosaurs it had a heavy club of bone at the end of its tail.

Talarurus facts

Lived: 85 million years ago

Found: Asia

Length: 5 metres

Armoured head

An ankylosaur's head was broad, with a big beak for biting off mouthfuls of plants. Plates of bone covered the head.

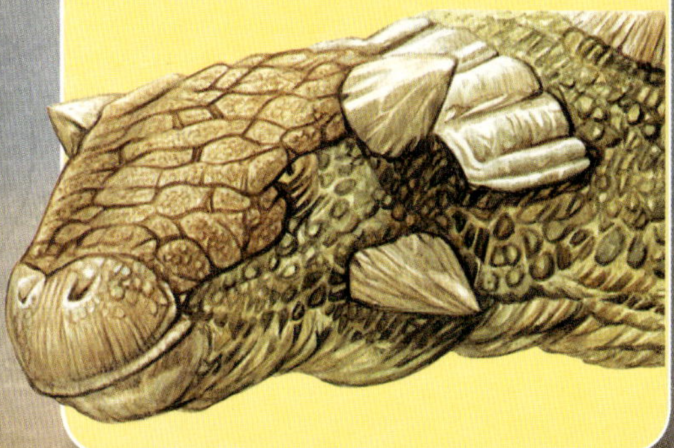

Pinacosaurus

This ankylosaur's head was only partly covered with bone. It lived in hot, dry areas of China and Mongolia.

Pinacosaurus facts

Lived: 80 million years ago

Found: Asia

Length: 5 metres

Pachycephalosaurs

These creatures are often called bone-heads or bone-headed dinosaurs. This is because they have a thick lump of bone on the head.

Built for speed

Pachycephalosaurs were probably fast movers. They stood upright and raced around on their long back legs.

Stygimoloch had lots of lumps and bumps on its head.

Stygimoloch

This is the only pachycephalosaur that had spikes on its head. These measured up to 15 centimetres long. Experts think that maybe only male *Stygimoloch* dinosaurs had spikes.

Stygimoloch facts

Lived: 70 million years ago

Found: North America

Length: 3 metres

Prenocephale

Prenocephale may have had a big head, but there was only a tiny brain inside. The bony dome was ringed with little spikes and lumps of bone.

Prenocephale facts

Lived: 70 million years ago

Found: Asia

Length: 2.5 metres

Stones

Pachycephalosaurs probably swallowed stones to help crush food in the stomach.

Pachycephalosaurus

This dinosaur was the largest of the bone-heads. The bony dome on top of its head was an amazing 25 centimetres thick.

Pachycephalosaurus facts

Lived: 70 million years ago

Found: North America

Length: 4.6 metres

Stegosaurs 1

The first stegosaurs lived about 170 million years ago. There were lots of different kinds and they lived in Africa, Asia, Europe and North America. The last stegosaurs died out about 90 million years ago.

Dacentrurus

This stegosaur had two rows of big bony spikes along its back and down to the tip of its tail.

Dacentrurus had a small head like other stegosaurs.

Scelidosaurus

Scelidosaurus came before the stegosaurs and was related to them. Its body was covered with lots of bony studs that made it hard to attack.

Scelidosaurus facts

Lived: 200 million years ago

Found: Europe

Length: 4 metres

Tiny heads

All stegosaurs had small heads. The head was about the same size as the head of a meat-eating dromaeosaur. At the front of the mouth was a hard beak for chopping mouthfuls of plants.

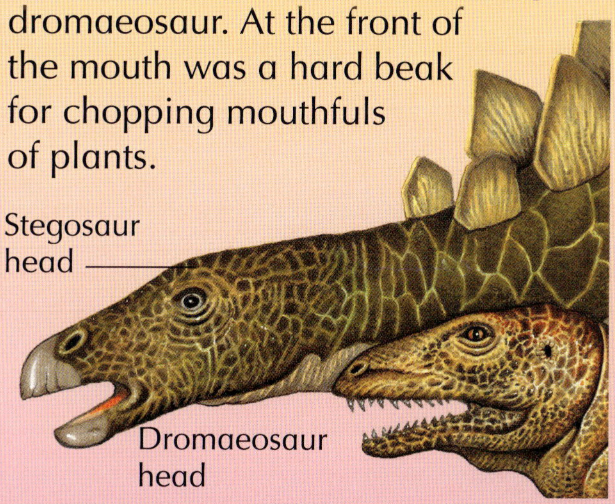

Dacentrurus facts

Lived: 155 million years ago

Found: Europe

Length: 5 metres

Kentrosaurus

Kentrosaurus was very well armoured. On its back were two rows of seven bony plates. Then came two rows of bony spines. And there was a big, sharp spike on each hip!

Kentrosaurus facts

Lived: 155 million years ago

Found: Africa

Length: 5 metres

Stegosaurs 2

Stegosaurs may have shown off their bony plates to attract mates. Or the plates may have helped control body heat.

Lexovisaurus

As well as bony plates, this stegosaur had a big spike sticking out from each shoulder.

Hip and shoulder spines

These sharp spines jutting out from the body helped the stegosaur protect itself from attackers.

Huayangosaurus

This was one of the earliest stegosaurs. It had teeth at the front of its mouth. Later stegosaurs did not.

Huayangosaurus facts

Lived: 165 million years ago

Found: Asia

Length: 4.5 metres

Lexovisaurus facts
Lived: 165 million years ago
Found: Europe
Length: 5 metres

Tuojiangosaurus facts
Lived: 155 million years ago
Found: Asia
Length: 7 metres

Tuojiangosaurus

Fifteen pairs of pointed bony plates lined the back of this Chinese stegosaur. Like other stegosaurs, it fed on plants such as ferns and cycads.

Stegosaurus

Stegosaurus was the biggest stegosaur. Lots of fossils have been found, so it is also the best known of its family.

The name *Stegosaurus* means 'roofed reptile'.

Dinosaur fact

Stegosaurus facts

Lived: 140 million years ago

Found: North America

Length: 9 metres

The skin covering the plates on a stegosaur's back may have flushed red with blood when the animal was excited or scared.

Fighting

Two males fight over a female *Stegosaurus*. They turn their bodies sideways to show off their full size.

Sting in the tail

Stegosaurus was a slow-moving plant-eater, if attacked it hit out with his tail.

Roof reptile
When fossils of this dinosaur were first found, experts thought that the bony plates lay flat, covering the animal's back like a turtle's shell. Later they realized that the plates actually stood upright.

Stegosaurus's plate pattern
Experts aren't sure how the bony plates were arranged. They may have been in one row, in pairs, or overlapping in a staggered row.

Stegoceras

These dinosaurs may have butted each other in the side when fighting for mates or leadership.

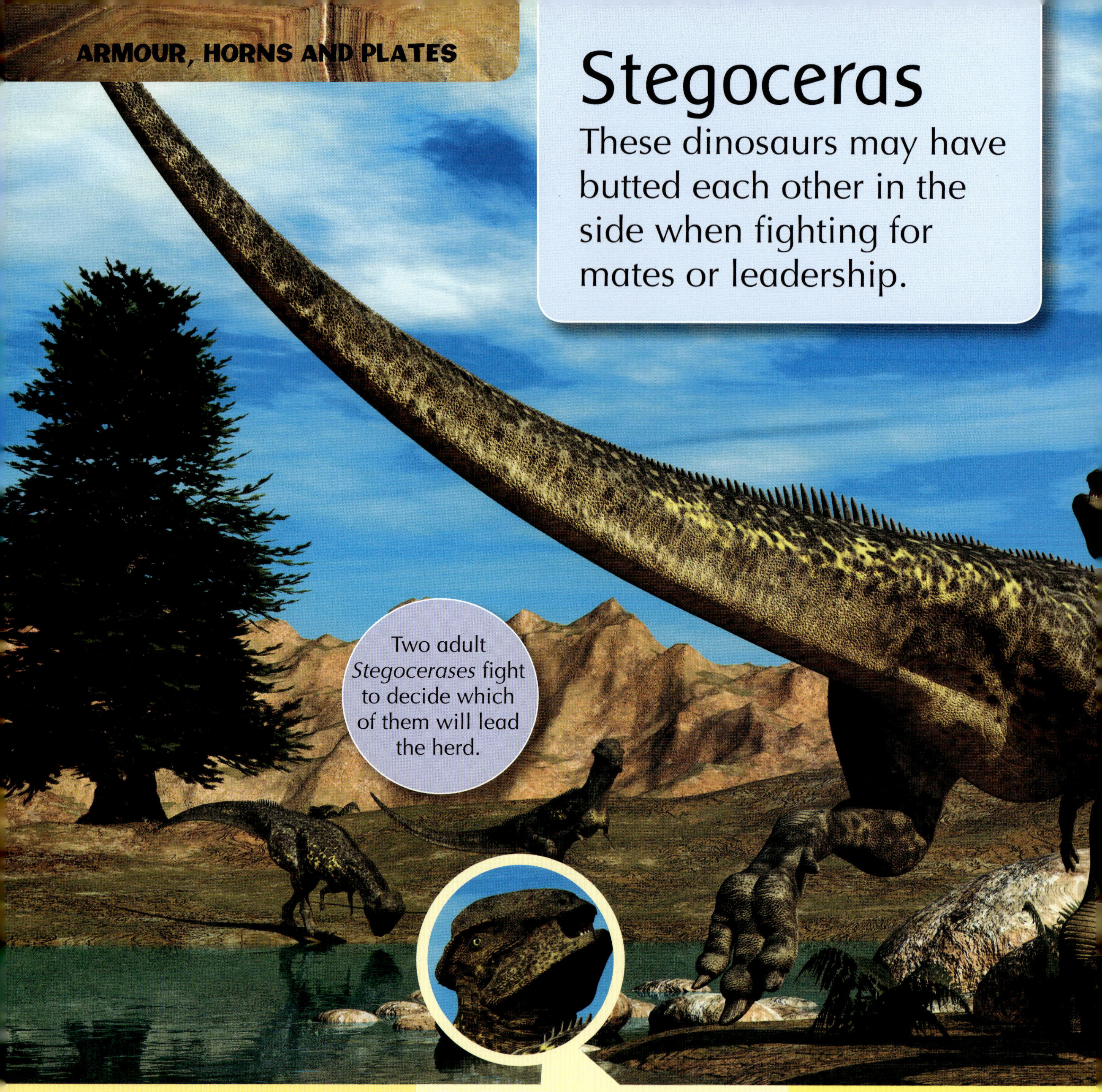

Two adult *Stegocerases* fight to decide which of them will lead the herd.

Stegoceras moved on its two long back legs, with its long tail held straight out behind it.

Stegoceras skull

The skull was up to 6 centimetres thick over the brain area. At the back of the skull was a ridge that was covered with knobs and lumps.

Sharp teeth

Stegoceras had lots of small, sharp teeth for cutting up tough plants. It may also have eaten some insects or other small creatures.

Hand-to-mouth feeding

Stegoceras probably grabbed or dug up plants with its strong hands and fingers and pulled them towards its mouth.

Head domes

A young *Stegoceras* dinosaur had a fairly flat head. The high bony dome grew bigger and bigger as the dinosaur grew up.

Ceratopsians 1

All ceratopsians had a parrot-like beak at the front of the mouth. They ranged from the size of a turkey to the size of an elephant.

Leptoceratops had a small, bony neck frill.

Leptoceratops

This small dinosaur had a slim body and could probably move quite fast.

Protoceratops

A nest of fossilized eggs laid by this dinosaur was found in the Gobi Desert in Mongolia. The eggs were about 20 centimetres long and arranged in a circle in a little dip in the sand.

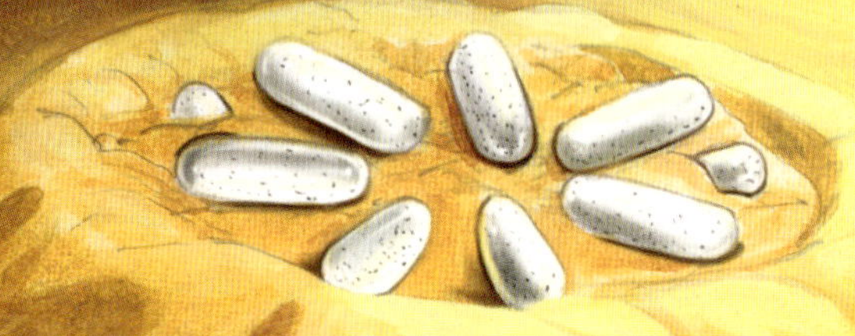

Protoceratops facts

Lived: 80 million years ago

Found: Asia

Length: 2.5 metres

Leptoceratops facts

Lived: 70 million years ago

Found: Australia, N. America

Length: 2 metres

Dinosaur beak

Psittacosaurus's beak looks a lot like a parrot's beak. The beak was covered with a tough material called horn.

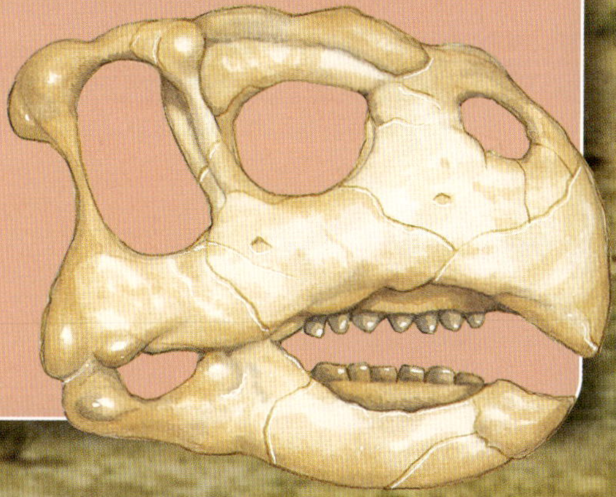

DID YOU KNOW?

Psittacosaurus means 'parrot lizard'. The dinosaur was given this name because of its beak.

Psittacosaurus

This dinosaur walked upright on its two back legs. It may have used its hands to gather plant food, which it cut through with its sharp beak.

Psittacosaurus facts

Lived: 130 million years ago

Found: Asia

Length: 2.5 metres

Ceratopsians 2

Some of these dinosaurs had very large, bony neck frills. The skin over the frill may have been brightly coloured and helped the dinosaur attract a mate.

DID YOU KNOW? Even a mighty tyrannosaur couldn't always win a battle with a huge horned ceratopsian.

Pachyrhinosaurus facts

Lived: 70 million years ago

Found: North America

Length: 6 metres

Pachyrhinosaurus

Pachyrhinosaurus had a bony lump on its nose as well as as a neck frill. We don't know if it had a horn too, because no complete skulls have yet been found.

Torosaurus

This amazing ceratopsian had the biggest skull of any animal that has ever lived on land. It measured up to 2.5 metres long.

Torosaurus facts

Lived: 70 million years ago

Found: North America

Length: 7.5 metres

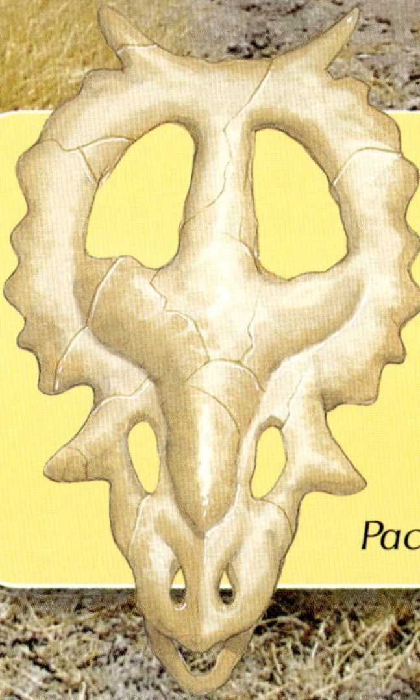

Skin-covered holes

The neck frills of ceratopsians had big holes in them. Otherwise, they would have been too heavy to carry around.

Pachyrhinosaurus skull

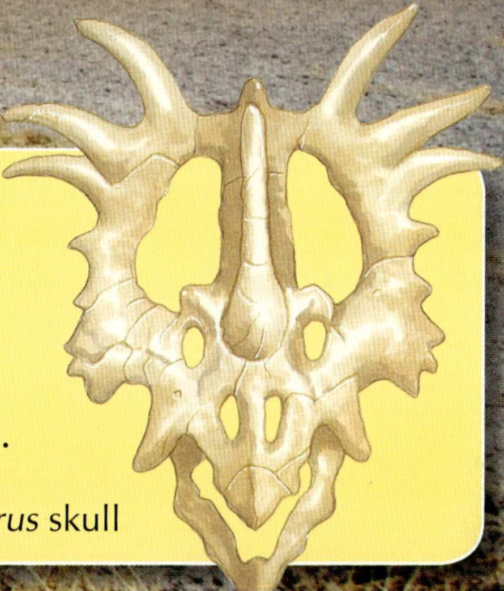

Styracosaurus skull

Triceratops

This dinosaur's neck frill was made of solid bone. The horns on top of its head were up to 1 metre long, but the nose horn was smaller.

The name *Triceratops* means 'three-horned face'.

Triceratops is the most famous of the ceratopsians, or horned dinosaurs.

Strong body

Triceratops had a big, chunky body, a short tail, and thick legs. It weighed about 10 tonnes and was strong enough to fight off even fierce hunters such as tyrannosaurs.

Plant-eater

Triceratops looked very fierce, but like other ceratopsians, it ate only plants. It bit off mouthfuls of leaves with its sharp beak.

Dinosaur fact

Triceratops facts

Lived: 70 million years ago

Found: North America

Length: 9 metres

Protecting the weak

Triceratops lived in a group, or herd, of animals. Young animals stayed in the centre of the group where they were safe from attackers.

Big battles

Triceratops probably fought over mates or who would lead the herd. They crashed their heads together and locked horns.

Dinosaur fact

Euoplocephalus facts

Lived: 70 million years ago

Found: North America

Length: 7 metres

Euoplocephalus

This dinosaur looked like a walking suit of armour. Only its underbelly was unprotected, so attackers would probably have had to flip it over in order to wound it.

Even *Euoplocephalus'* eyelids had a layer of bone above them!

Euoplocephalus lived in the forests and it may have moved around in herds.

Bonehead

Euoplocephalus was covered in bony knobs and plates that protected its body. It had four horns around its head, and spines down its back.

More brawn than brain

From the size of its brain in comparison with its body, scientists think that *Euoplocephalus* was among the less intelligent of the dinosaurs.

Warning sign

If threatened, this dinosaur would probably have swung the bony club at the end of its tail to warn its enemies to stay away.

Sturdy giant

Euoplocephalus had four short, sturdy legs. Its rear legs were larger than its front legs.

Duck-bills and other dinosaurs

Many new kinds of plant-eating dinosaurs, such as duck-bills and iguanodonts, appeared in the Jurassic and Cretaceous periods. All had a bony beak for biting into plants and strong teeth for chewing.

Ornithopods – the 'bird-feet' dinosaurs

These dinosaurs are called 'bird-feet dinosaurs because they walked upright and on tiptoe like birds. There were many different kinds of ornithopods all over the world.

DID YOU KNOW?

Many ornithopods lived in big groups, called herds, made up of thousands of animals.

'Different teeth' dinosaurs

These dinosaurs were also called heterodontosaurs. They had three kinds of teeth shaped for cutting, chewing and stabbing.

Parksosaurus

Different sizes

The smallest ornithopods were only about 2 metres long. The biggest were 10–20 metres long.

Iguanodon 10 metres long.

'High ridge teeth' dinosaurs

These dinosaurs were also called hypsilophodonts. *Parksosaurus* was a hypsilophodont.

Duck-billed dinosaurs

These dinosaurs are known as duck-bills because of their beaks, which looked like a duck's beak. They are also called hadrosaurs, which means 'big lizards'. *Edmontosaurus* and *Parasaurolophus* were duck-bills.

Beaks

Ornithopod dinosaurs had bony beaks at the front of their jaws. These were covered with a hard material called horn. They were just right for biting off mouthfuls of plants.

Edmontosaurus

Hypsilophodon

Iguanodonts

The name of this group of dinosaurs means 'iguana teeth'. They got this name because people thought their teeth looked like those of iguana lizards. *Iguanodon* is the best known iguanodont.

Heterodontosaurs

These dinosaurs were the first of the ornithopods. They appeared about 220 million years ago and were all small plant-eaters that walked upright on two legs.

Three types of teeth

At the front of the mouth, behind the beak, were small, sharp teeth for biting. Then came two pairs of tusk-like teeth. At the back of the mouth were lots of wider teeth for chewing food.

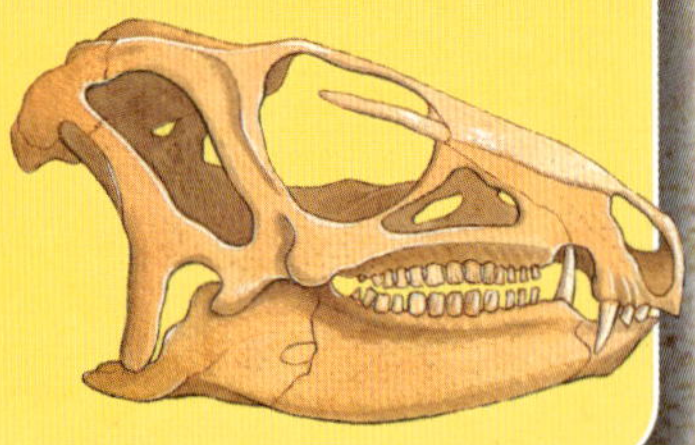

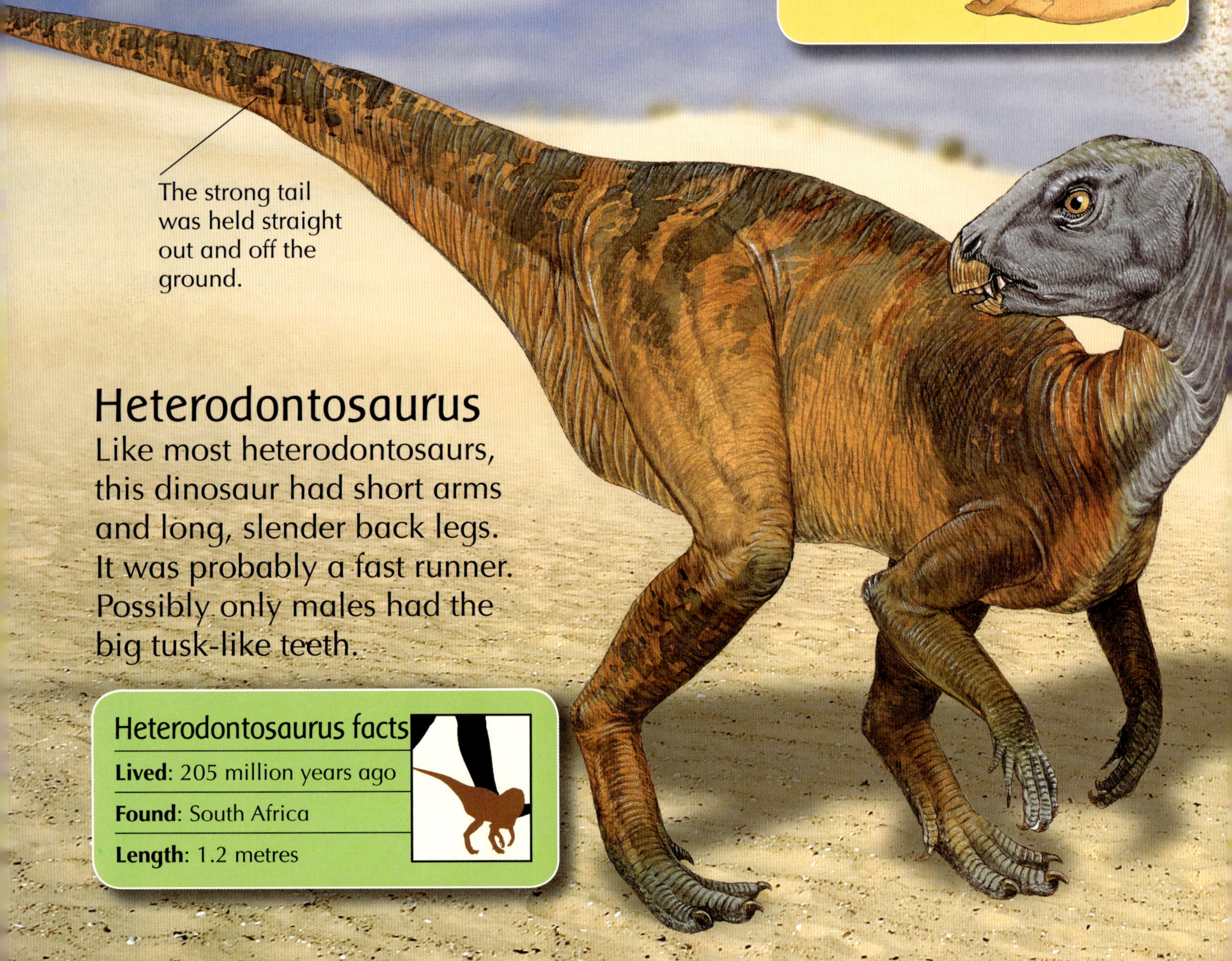

Heterodontosaurus

Like most heterodontosaurs, this dinosaur had short arms and long, slender back legs. It was probably a fast runner. Possibly only males had the big tusk-like teeth.

Heterodontosaurus facts

Lived: 205 million years ago

Found: South Africa

Length: 1.2 metres

Abrictosaurus

This dinosaur had no long tusk-like teeth. It may have been a female *Heterodontosaurus* and not a separate species.

Abrictosaurus facts

Lived: 205 million years ago

Found: South Africa

Length: 1.2 metres

Pisanosaurus

Pisanosaurus was one of the first heterodontosaurs and one of the earliest dinosaurs. Only some of its bones have been found, not a whole skeleton.

Dinosaurs with cheek pouches

As a heterodontosaur chewed, the food collected in its fleshy cheek pouches. The dinosaur then used its tongue to move the food back to its jaws.

Pisanosaurus facts

Lived: 220 million years ago

Found: South America

Length: 90 cm (uncertain)

Hypsilophodonts 1

These dinosaurs lived like antelopes and deer today. They moved around in herds, feeding on low-growing plants.

Hypsilophodon

Hypsilophodon had lots of ridged teeth, and cheek pouches for holding partly chewed food.

Built for speed

Hypsilophodonts were fast movers. They could probably run at up to 40 kilometres per hour for a short time.

Horsetails

Hypsilophodon ate these plants. They first grew more than 400 million years ago and still grow today.

DID YOU KNOW?

The biggest hypsilophodont was about 4 metres long.

Hypsilophodon facts

Lived: 120 million years ago

Found: Europe, N. America

Length: 2.4 metres

Fulgurotherium facts

Lived: 130 million years ago

Found: Australia

Length: 2 metres

Fulgurotherium

This dinosaur lived very far south. It may have moved north in winter to escape the icy weather.

Thescelosaurus

This was one of the last of the hypsilophodonts. It lived right at the end of the age of reptiles.

Thescelosaurus facts

Lived: 70 million years ago

Found: North America

Length: 4 metres

Hypsilophodonts 2

These dinosaurs get their name from their strange-shaped teeth. The teeth had ridges on them which helped break down food as the animal chewed. Cows chew like this.

Dryosaurus

Like other hypsilophodonts, *Dryosaurus* probably lived in herds. They may have travelled long distances to find plants to eat.

Agilisaurus

Experts aren't sure if this dinosaur is a hypsilophodont or one of a new family of dinosaurs.

Agilisaurus facts

Lived: 165 million years ago

Found: Asia

Length: 1 metre

A diet of plants

A hypsilophodont bit off leaves with the bony beak at the front of its mouth.

Dryosaurus had five fingers on each hand.

Dryosaurus facts

Lived: 150 million years ago

Found: Africa, North America

Length: 4 metres

DID YOU KNOW? Experts once thought that hypsilophodonts could climb trees. But now they think the dinosaurs lived on the ground.

Parksosaurus

This was one of the last of the hypsilophodonts. Its tail was strong and stiff and the dinosaur held its tail straight out behind to help keep its balance as it ran.

Parksosaurus facts

Lived: 65 million years ago

Found: North America

Length: 2.4 metres

Iguanodonts 1

These dinosaurs lived like cows and deer do today. They moved around in herds and spent most of their time feeding on large amounts of plant material.

Camptosaurus facts
Lived: 150 million years ago
Found: Europe, N. America
Length: 6 metres

Camptosaurus

Like other iguanodonts, this dinosaur had strong teeth behind its sharp beak. It could even chew tough conifer needles.

Conifer forest

Conifer trees came before flowering plants and their needle-like leaves were an important food for dinosaurs.

Muttaburrasaurus

This dinosaur looked a lot like *Iguanodon*, but it had a small lump of bone on its nose. Also, its teeth were shaped for cutting through plants rather than grinding them into pieces.

Muttaburrasaurus facts

Lived: 110 million years ago

Found: Australia

Length: 7 metres

Ouranosaurus facts

Lived: 110 million years ago

Found: Africa

Length: 7 metres

Ouranosaurus

Ouranosaurus had a row of spines along its back. These were covered with skin. This 'sail' might have been brightly coloured to scare off meat-eating dinosaurs.

Iguanodonts 2

Later species of this type of dinosaur were different from the first iguanodonts in several ways. For example, they had stronger backs, more teeth and three toes instead of four.

Probactrosaurus

Probactrosaurus had a long, narrow head and lots of broad teeth for chewing. If teeth wore down and fell out, new ones grew to replace them.

DID YOU KNOW?

Iguanodonts may have been able to stand on their back legs to reach food higher up.

Tenontosaurus

This big plant-eater looked very much like *Iguanodon*. The teeth of a meat-eating *Deinonychus* have been found with the bones of *Tenontosaurus*, so it may have been the victim of predator attacks.

Tenontosaurus facts

Lived: 115 million years ago

Found: North America

Length: 7 metres

Probactrosaurus facts

Lived: 100 million years ago

Found: Asia

Length: 6 metres

The tail was held very straight and didn't move around much.

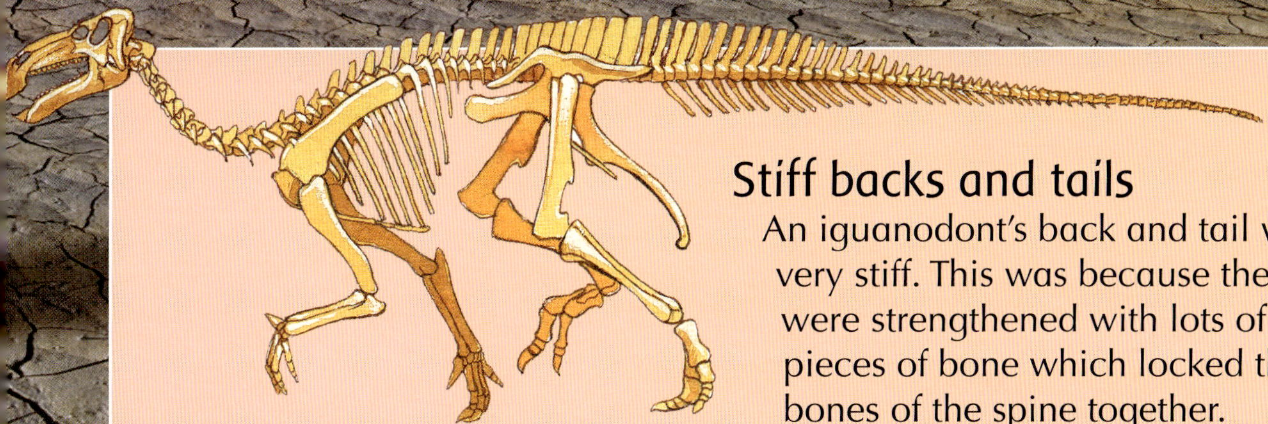

Stiff backs and tails

An iguanodont's back and tail were very stiff. This was because they were strengthened with lots of thin pieces of bone which locked the bones of the spine together.

Dinosaur fact

Iguanodon facts

Lived: 130 million years ago

Found: Asia, Europe, N. America

Length: 10 metres

Iguanodon

This dinosaur was named *Iguanodon*, which means 'iguana teeth' because its teeth looked like those of the iguana lizard.

Iguanodon was only the second dinosaur ever to be named.

Iguanodon had four clawed fingers and a big spiky thumb.

Horse head

Iguanodon was a big animal with a long, stiff tail. It had a long head like a horse's and its jaws were filled with lots of sharp teeth.

Using the thumb

Iguanodon could have used its thumb spike like a dagger to defend itself from meat-eating dinosaurs. It could also bend its little finger across its hand to help it hold on to things, such as twigs and leaves.

Ground to a pulp

Using the strong beak at the front of its mouth, *Iguanodon* bit off leaves and twigs to eat. It chewed its food for a long time until it was just a mushy pulp.

Two legs or four

This dinosaur could walk upright on its two back legs or on all fours. It could run at speeds of up to 19 kilometres per hour.

Hadrosaurs 1

These dinosaurs are also called 'duck-bills' because they have a beak like a duck's. They were one of the last types of dinosaur and lived until the end of the age of the reptiles.

Saurolophus

This hadrosaur had a long bony spike on the back of its head. This may have been covered with a flap of skin, making a bag that made the dinosaur's honking calls louder.

Hadrosaurus

A skeleton of this dinosaur was found in the USA in 1857. It was the first nearly complete dinosaur skeleton ever found.

Hadrosaurus facts

Lived: 75 million years ago	
Found: North America	
Length: 9 metres	

Saurolophus facts

Lived: 70 million years ago

Found: Asia, North America

Length: 12 metres

Wide duck-like mouths

It's easy to see why these dinosaurs are called duck-bills. The beak at the front of the mouth was wide and flat. It was covered with a hard material called horn.

The head crest may have made the dinosaur's calls louder.

Lambeosaurus

Both male and female *Lambeosaurus* had bony crests on their heads. The males also had a spike of solid bone behind the crest.

Lambeosaurus facts

Lived: 70 million years ago

Found: North America

Length: 9 metres

Hadrosaurs 2

These dinosaurs probably spent most of their time on all fours, as they moved around feeding on plants. But they could rear up on their strong back legs to run away from predators.

Tsintaosaurus facts

Lived: 70 million years ago

Found: Asia

Length: 10 metres

Tsintaosaurus

This big Chinese hadrosaur had a spiky head crest. The spike often measured up to 1 metre long.

Leaellynasaura

This dinosaur may have hibernated for some of the winter. This meant that its body slowed right down as it slept to save energy. It woke up when warmer spring days arrived.

Loud calls

The head crests were hollow inside. They may have acted like echo chambers to make the dinosaurs' calls louder.

DID YOU KNOW?

A hadrosaur had as many as 1,600 teeth packed tightly in its jaws.

Corythosaurus

This dinosaur lived around swamps at the edge of forests. It may have been able to wade through water or even swim.

Corythosaurus facts

Lived: 80 million years ago

Found: North America

Length: 9 metres

Parasaurolophus may have moved around in herds.

This dinosaur was one of the largest hadrosaurs.

A cool head

Scientists think that the crest on *Parasaurolophus's* head may have helped keep its brain cool. It may also have helped other animals identify the dinosaur and know whether it was male or female.

Long crest

Parasaurolophus had a notch, or dip, in its back, right where the crest would touch it if it leaned its head backward. This may have been because the crest on its head was extremely long and as big as the rest of its skull.

Parasaurolophus

This dinosaur had a long, hollow, bony crest on its head, which it may have used to make a foghorn-like sound.

Dinosaur fact

Parasaurolophus facts

Lived: 75 million years ago

Found: North America

Length: 10 metres

Strong legs

Parasaurolophus could walk and run fairly fast on its two strong back legs. It also spent a lot of time on all four legs, especially when feeding.

Chewy food

Like other hadrosaurs, *Parasaurolophus* fed on a mixture of tough twigs, pine needles and softer leaves. Its jaws could move enough to grind up its food with its teeth, which were constantly replaced as they wore down.

A *Maiasaura* keeps an eye on its nest of eggs.

These big plant-eaters lived in large herds of as many as 10,000 animals.

Good mothers

Maiasaura mothers stayed near their eggs to protect them from predators. When the young hatched, their mothers brought them food until they were big enough to leave the nest.

Feast

Each animal in the herd needed to find as much as 90 kg of plants a day.

Maiasaura

The name *Maiasaura* means 'good mother lizard'. Nests and fossilized eggs belonging to this dinosaur have been found, so we know a lot about its nesting habits.

Dinosaur fact

Maiasaura facts
Lived: 80 million years ago
Found: North America
Length: 9 metres

Maiasaura nest

The nest was a hollow in the ground and measured about 2 metres across. The mother dinosaur laid about 25 eggs, each about as big as a grapefruit.

At the nest site

Maiasaura was too big to sit on its eggs. It covered them with plants to keep them warm. When the young hatched they were about 30 centimetres long.

Dinosaur fact

Lesothosaurus facts

Lived: 200 million years ago

Found: South Africa

Length: 1 metre

Lesothosaurus couldn't reach up high, so it would have fed on low-growing plants or dug up plant roots with its hands.

Small but swift

This dinosaur had long back legs and was probably a fast runner. Its arms were short and it had five fingers on each hand which it could use for grabbing and digging for food.

Summer sleep

Two *Lesothosaurus* skeletons were found curled up together in a burrow. Experts think they may have crept in there to sleep through the hot summer months.

Lesothosaurus

Lesothosaurus was a plant-eater and had sharp pointed front teeth as well as bigger teeth for chewing.

A group of *Lesothosaurus* dinosaurs stop to feed.

Leaf-eater

The body and legs of this dinosaur look very much like those of a meat-eating dinosaur. But its head, bony beak and chewing teeth show that it was a plant-eater.

Dog-sized dinosaur

Lesothosaurus probably lived in groups. The dinosaurs ran across the hot, dry plains of Africa, searching for food. A full-grown adult was about the size of a dog.

Life in the air

At the time when dinosaurs lived on land, other kinds of reptile flew in the sky. These flying reptiles were called pterosaurs. They were the first vertebrates, animals with backbones, to take to life in the air. Pterosaurs appeared just after the first dinosaurs, about 225 million years ago.

Flying reptiles

There were many kinds of pterosaur. Some were as small as a blackbird today. The biggest was the size of a small plane – it was the largest flying creature that ever lived.

Wings of skin

A pterosaur's wings were made of skin and strengthened by thin strips of muscle. The wing was attached along each side of the pterosaur's body.

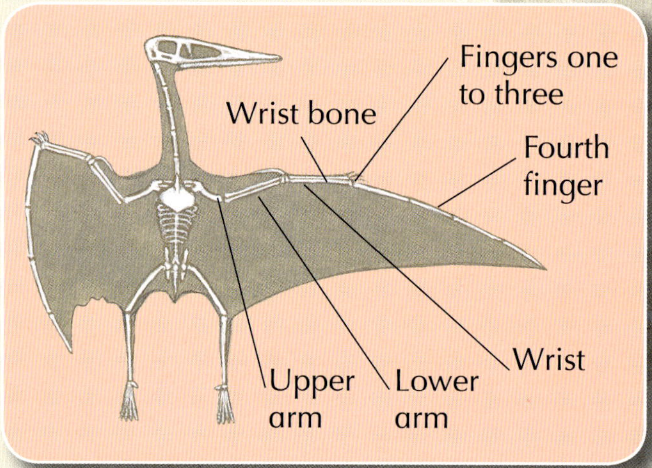

Long fingers

The wings were supported by the bones of the arms, hands and fingers. The top of the wing was attached to the very long fourth finger.

Different foods

Pterosaurs fed in different ways. Some flew over the sea, scooping fish from the water. Others snapped up insects in the air or hunted over land.

Soar or dart?

Some pterosaurs could glide for long distances, like sea birds today. Others had shorter wings and could twist and turn as they hunted prey.

DID YOU KNOW?

The name *pterosaur* means 'winged lizard'.

Wing muscles

Pterosaurs had to have strong muscles to move their wings up and down with.

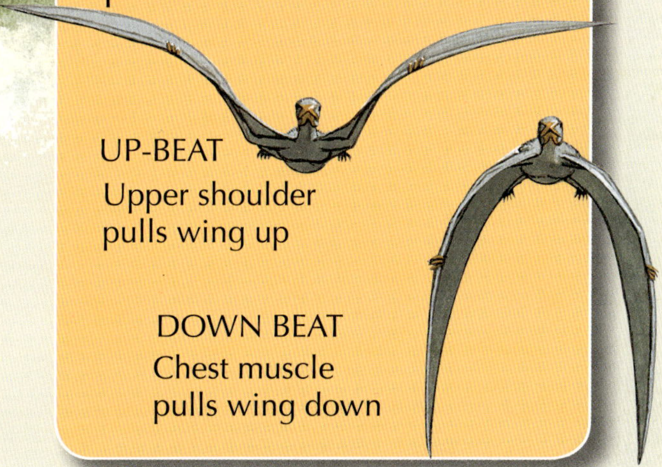

Triassic pterosaurs

There were two types of pterosaurs. The rhamphorhynchs came first. Later came the pterodactyls. All the pterosaurs on this page were rhamphorhynchs, with long tails and short necks.

Where did pterosaurs come from?

Pterosaurs may be related to gliding lizards similar to *Sharrovipteryx* (above), which lived in Asia.

Peteinosaurus

This was one of the earliest pterosaurs and it was about the same size as a pigeon. It probably caught insects such as dragonflies.

Peteinosaurus facts

Lived: 220 million years ago

Found: Europe

Wingspan: 60 centimetres

Pterosaurs and birds

A pterosaur's wings were made of skin and supported by its finger bones. A bird's wings are supported by the arm bones and covered with feathers.

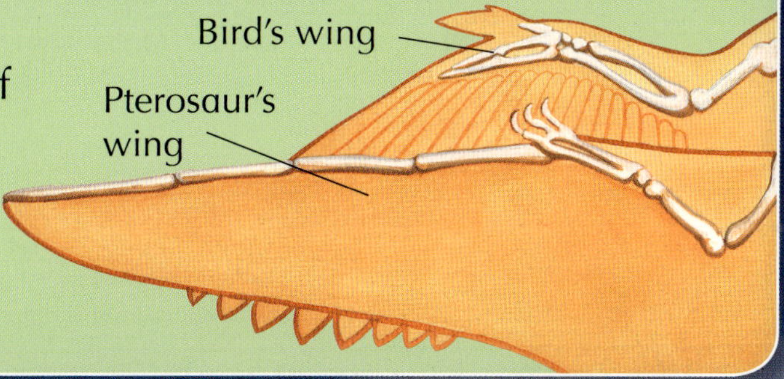

Preondactylus

This pterosaur was about the size of a blackbird. It had long, narrow jaws lined with lots of sharp teeth and probably fed on fish as well as insects.

Preondactylus facts

Lived: 220 million years ago

Found: Europe

Wingspan: 45 centimetres

DID YOU KNOW?

Pterosaurs were flying in the skies 75 million years before birds. The two groups come from different ancestors.

Dinosaur fact

Eudimorphodon facts

Lived: 220 million years ago

Found: Europe

Wingspan: 1 metre

Eudimorphodon

Like all the early pterosaurs, this one was a rhamphorhynch. It had two types of teeth – sharp fangs at the front of the jaws and smaller, pointed teeth further back.

Eudimorphodon measured 70 cm from its beak to the tip of its tail.

Fossils of this pterosaur have been found with fish scales in the stomach area.

Skull

Large holes in this pterosaur's skull made it lighter. This was important for a flying creature. It had 58 teeth in its upper jaw and 56 in the lower jaw.

Fine flier

With its long wings, *Eudimorphodon* was probably a good flier. Between flights, it could cling to to a cliff ledge or a tree using the strong claws at the top of each wing.

Fish for supper

This pterosaur may also have flown low over the water looking for food. It then swooped down and seized its prey. Its sharp teeth were just right for holding on to slippery fish.

Diving for fish

Eudimorphodon may have caught its food by diving into the water. It grabbed its fishy prey and then came back to the surface.

Jurassic pterosaurs of Europe

In the Jurassic period, pterosaurs began to get bigger and change in shape. They became more like the later pterodactyls.

Pterosaur heads ...

The first rhamphorhynchs had a short head, stubby neck and lots of teeth. The later pterodactyls had a long neck and beak, and few or no teeth.

Dorygnathus

This pterosaur had amazing teeth. They jutted out of its mouth to make a kind of spiky cage for trapping fish.

Dorygnathus facts

Lived: 190 million years ago

Found: Europe

Wingspan: 1 metre

Scaphognathus was one of the first fossil pterosaurs ever found.

Scaphognathus

This pterosaur had a short head and rounded nose. Its teeth were long and sharp. There were about 18 in the top jaw and 10 in the lower jaw.

Scaphognathus facts

Lived: 150 million years ago

Found: Europe

Wingspan: 90 centimetres

… and tails

Rhamphorhynchs had a long, thin bony tail that was quite stiff except at the base. Most were tipped with a flap of skin. Pterodactyls had a much shorter tail, made of just a few bones.

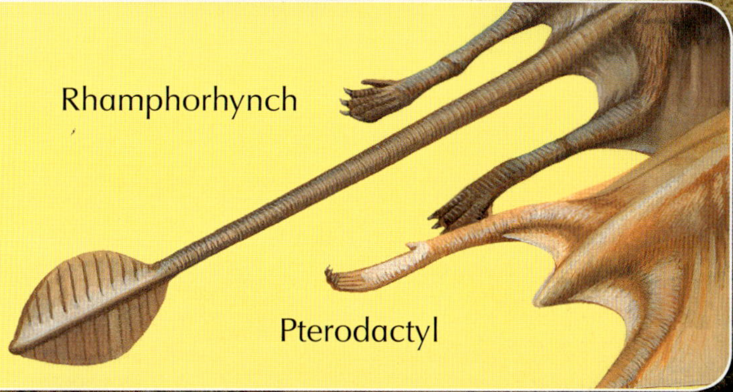

Dinosaur fact

Dimorphodon facts

Lived: 205 million years ago

Found: Europe

Wingspan: 1.4 metres

Dimorphodon lived about 205 million years ago in England.

Take-off

Dimorphodon had strong claws on its wings. It probably couldn't take off from the ground, but its claws helped it climb onto rocks or trees, where it could jump off into the air.

Walking pterosaur

Dimorphodon could stand up with its legs under its body and walk upright.

Dimorphodon

Dimorphodon belonged to the rhamphorhynch group and had a long tail, a big head and sharp teeth.

Dimorphodon's beak may have been brightly coloured, just like a hornbill's or puffin's beak today.

Or it could use the claws on its wings as front feet and scurry on all fours.

Toothy hunter

Dimorphodon probably hunted fish, insects, lizards, worms and other small creatures. It had two kinds of teeth. There were large peg-like teeth at the front of its jaws and smaller, sharp teeth behind them.

A smooth flier

Wide wings and a long trailing tail helped this pterosaur glide smoothly through the air. *Dimorphodon* also had very strong, well-developed legs, unlike most pterosaurs.

The pterodactyls arrive

The pterodactyls were the second group of pterosaurs. They first appeared in the late Jurassic period and lived until the end of the Cretaceous period.

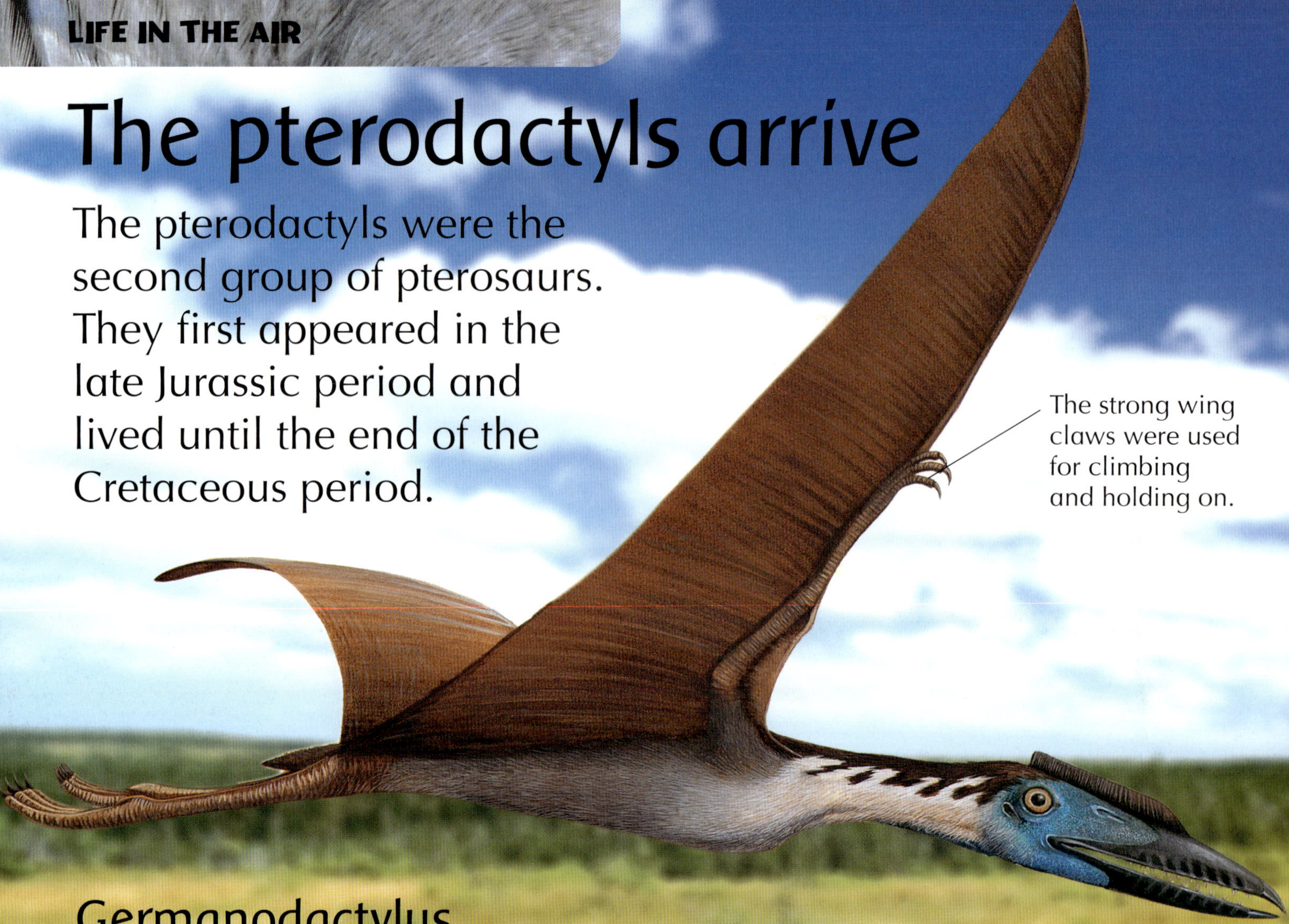

Germanodactylus

An early pterodactyl, *Germanodactylus* had a longer beak and fewer teeth than the rhamphorhynch pterosaurs.

Germanodactylus facts

Lived: 150 million years ago

Found: Europe

Wingspan: 1.35 metres

Hollow bones

Flying animals need to be light. Many of the pterosaur's bones were hollow inside. They were criss-crossed with little bony rods to make them stronger.

Furry bodies

Fossils show that a pterosaur's head and body may have been covered with short hair. There would have been no hair on the wings or tail.

DID YOU KNOW?

Pterodactyls may have slept hanging upside down from branches, like bats do today.

Gallodactylus had a long narrow beak.

Gallodactylus

This pterosaur had a crest on the back of its head instead of on its beak like earlier pterosaurs. It is possible that the crest may have helped it steer while in the air.

Gallodactylus facts

Lived: 150 million years ago

Found: Europe

Wingspan: 1 metre

Unusual Jurassic pterosaurs

There were still a few kinds of rhamphorhynchs around in the Jurassic period, living alongside the pterodactyls. Two of the most unusual were *Anurognathus* and *Sordes*.

Taking off

To take off from a cliff ledge, a pterosaur probably pushed with its hands and feet to launch itself into the air. Then it opened its wings to stop itself falling further and began to fly.

Sordes

The name of this pterosaur means 'hairy devil'. Fossils show that it had a thick coat of long fur on its head and body, and even some thinner hair on its wings.

Sordes facts

Lived: 150 million years ago

Found: Asia

Wingspan: 60 centimetres

Anurognathus facts

Lived: 150 million years ago

Found: Europe

Wingspan: 50 centimetres

Anurognathus

This little pterosaur was a rhamphorhynch, but it had a short tail like a pterodactyl. It had small sharp teeth and may have snapped up insects in the air like swifts do today.

Crest of a wave

Sometimes pterosaurs had to take off from the water. They may have leapt into the air from the crest of a wave, or pushed off with their feet.

Pterodactylus

There were several different kinds of *Pterodactylus*, which lived from about 160 to 145 million years ago. Fossils have been found in parts of Europe and in Africa.

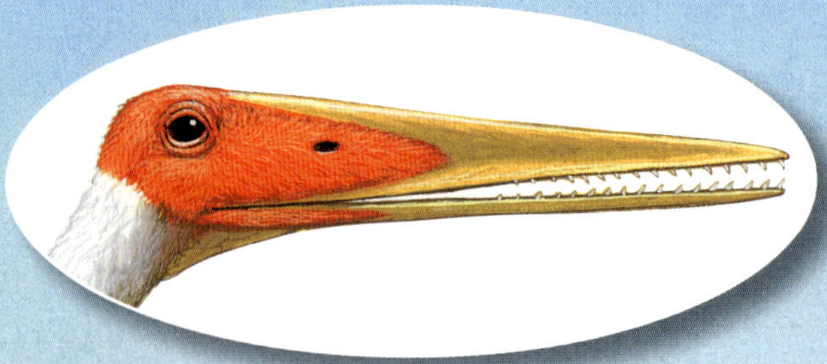

Beaks and teeth

Some kinds of *Pterodactylus* had evenly spaced teeth. Others had more teeth at the front of the beak and none at the back.

Many sizes

Some kinds of *Pterodactylus* were the size of a blackbird. Others were giants with a wingspan of 2.5 metres.

Pterodactylus facts

Lived: 160–145 million years ago

Found: Europe and Africa

Wingspan: 36–250 centimetres

In the air and at rest

Pterodactylus had very long, narrow wings and could probably fly well. It may have rested hanging upside down from its claws on tree branches.

Creature features

Pterodactylus had a short tail and a long neck. There were big holes in its skull bones, making the skull very light.

Feeding young

Young *Pterodactylus* could fly, but they may not have been able to catch food. A parent may have regurgitated or 'brought up' food for its young.

Early Cretaceous pterosaurs

By the Cretaceous period there were no rhamphorhynch pterosaurs left. But there were many kinds of pterodactyls and they were spreading all over the world.

Ornithodesmus

This was one of the first really big pterosaurs. It had an unusual spoon-shaped beak and lots of short sharp teeth. These were ideal for spiking and trapping fish.

Ornithodesmus facts

Lived: 130 million years ago

Found: Europe

Wingspan: 5 metres

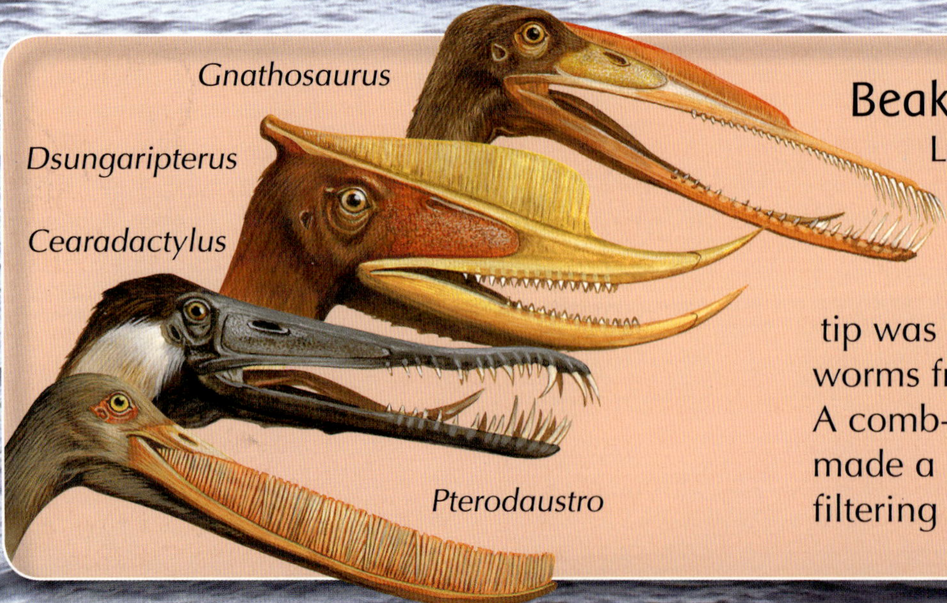

Beaks and food

Long thin teeth were used to grab fish or other small prey. A beak with a pointed tip was just right for digging worms from the sea bed. A comb-like fringe of teeth made a perfect sieve for filtering food.

Where did pterosaurs live?

Many pterosaurs fed on fish and probably lived near water. Fossils have been found near oceans, lakes, rivers and swamps. Some may also have lived in forests, or even in deserts, but we don't know for sure.

Anhanguera

Anhanguera had a flexible neck to grab food from the surface of the water with, but small, weak legs that would have made walking difficult.

Anhanguera facts

Lived: 120 million years ago

Found: South America

Wingspan: 4 metres

Cretaceous specialized feeders

Many pterosaurs fed on fish. But some kinds of pterosaur had special beaks for feeding on other sea creatures, such as shellfish, worms and shrimps.

Pterodaustro

This pterosaur had a fringe of thin teeth like the bristles of a brush on its lower jaw. With these, it could sweep tiny shrimps and other food from the water.

Pterodaustro facts

Lived: 140 million years ago

Found: South America

Wingspan: 1.3 metres

DID YOU KNOW?

There were about 1,000 closely packed bristly teeth in *Pterodaustro's* lower jaw.

Pterosaur nurseries

Pterosaurs probably laid eggs, and they may have nested in groups. The parents could have left their young together on the clifftops while they went to find food for them.

Dsungaripterus facts
Lived: 145 million years ago
Found: Asia
Wingspan: 3 metres

Dsungaripterus

This large pterosaur had a beak like a pair of tongs. It could have poked the pointed tips into sand or cracks in the rocks and pulled out food, such as worms and shellfish.

Pterodaustro is nicknamed the flamingo pterosaur!

More pterosaurs

Pterosaurs had to fly to find food so their wings were very important. They probably took great care of their wings, folding them away when resting. They kept them clean, too, picking out any dirt with their claws or teeth.

First pterosaur fossil

This was found in Germany in 1784. Experts decided it was the fossil of a flying reptile and named it *Pterodactyle*, which means 'wing finger'.

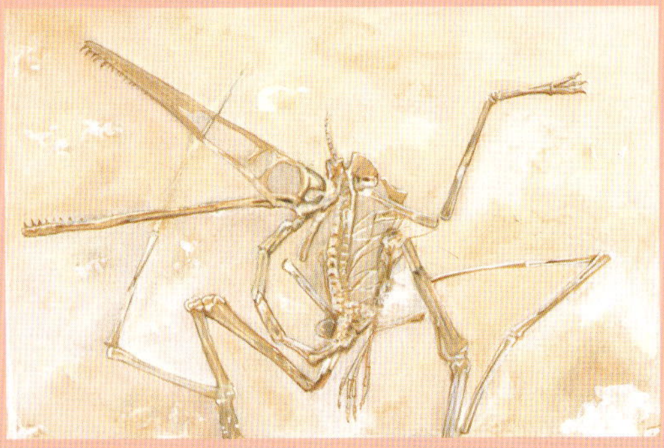

Tropeognathus

Tropeognathus had a crest on the top and bottom of its beak. It may have used these to steady its beak when feeding in water, or showed them off to attract mates at breeding time.

Tropeognathus facts

Lived: 120 million years ago

Found: South America

Wingspan: 6 metres

Pterosaur head crests

Crests may have been brightly coloured to help pterosaurs attract mates. They may also have helped keep the animal steady in the air.

Pteranodon ingens

Germanodactylus

Tapejara

Pteranodon

Pteranodon had very long wings. From tip to tip, they measured more than four grown-up people lying head to toe.

Pteranodon facts

Lived: 85 million years ago

Found: Europe, N. America, Asia

Wingspan: 8 metres

Pteranodon had huge wings but weighed only 1.8 kilograms.

Sea cliffs

Pterosaurs such as *Pteranodon* probably took off into the air from high sea cliffs.

Dinosaur fact

Quetzalcoatlus facts

Lived: 70 million years ago

Found: North America

Wingspan: 11 metres

Quetzalcoatlus probably had excellent eyesight.

This amazing pterosaur was probably the biggest flying creature that has ever lived.

The pterosaur 'vulture'?

This flying giant may have fed the way vultures do today. As it flew over land, it looked for dead or dying animals. If it spotted something, it landed and fed on the creature with its sharp beak.

Strong beak

Quetzalcoatlus may have searched rivers and lakes for food, and chopped up crabs and other shellfish with its strong beak.

Quetzalcoatlus

Quetzalcoatlus was as big as a small plane. Its wings measured at least 11 metres from tip to tip.

Noisy

We don't know if pterosaurs made loud squawking noises, as seagulls do today. Perhaps they made clacking sounds with their beaks or clapped their large wings.

Fuzzy fur

Quetzalcoatlus means 'feathered serpent', but as far as we know the pterosaur did not have feathers. Its body may have been covered with fuzzy fur or hair-like scales.

The teeming seas

No dinosaurs lived in the sea, although some may have been able to splash their way across a lake or river. But the seas were full of other creatures, such as fish and shellfish. There were also several kinds of large sea-dwelling reptiles, including plesiosaurs, pliosaurs and ichthyosaurs.

Oceans in the age of dinosaurs

Large, swimming reptiles ruled the seas during the age of the dinosaurs. All were hunters, and chased fish and other sea creatures to eat.

Taking a breath

Sea-living reptiles did not have gills like fish. So they had to come to the surface regularly to breathe.

Other sea creatures

All these creatures lived alongside sea-living reptiles. Ammonites were common but are now extinct.

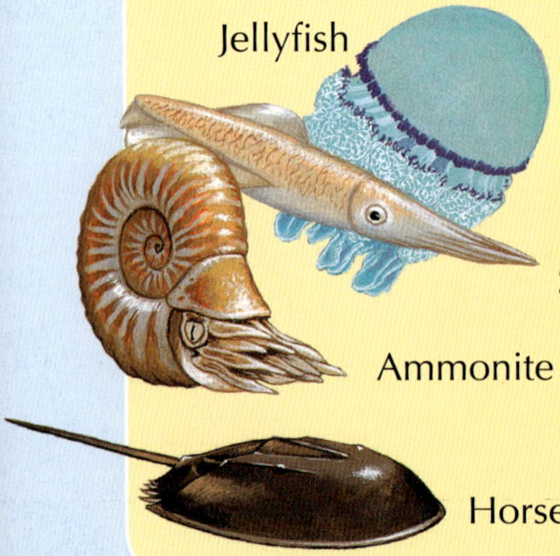

Ocean reptiles

Ichthyosaurs, pliosaurs and plesiosaurs became extinct at the same time as the dinosaurs. They died out forever. But other reptiles such as turtles still live in our seas.

Seafood

There had been fish living in the sea for 300 million years before the dinosaurs appeared. Sharks had already been the top predators in the ocean for more than 200 million years.

Flippers to paddle

These swimming reptiles had bodies shaped to speed easily through the water. They had flippers instead of legs.

DID YOU KNOW?

Ichthyosaurs probably gave birth to live young in the water instead of laying eggs like land reptiles.

Nothosaurs

Nothosaurs were the first big sea-living reptiles. They had webbed feet instead of flippers and may have spent some of their time on land.

Lariosaurus

This reptile's feet were better for walking than swimming. It may have done some hunting on the sea shore.

Ceresiosaurus

This nothosaur had very long toes on its feet. It probably swam by moving its long body and tail from side to side and making rowing movements with its front feet.

Ceresiosaurus facts
Lived: 225 million years ago
Found: Europe
Length: 4 metres

Lariosaurus facts

Lived: 225 million years ago

Found: Europe

Length: 60 centimetres

Pistosaurus

Pistosaurus's legs were like flippers. It probably used these to push itself through the water.

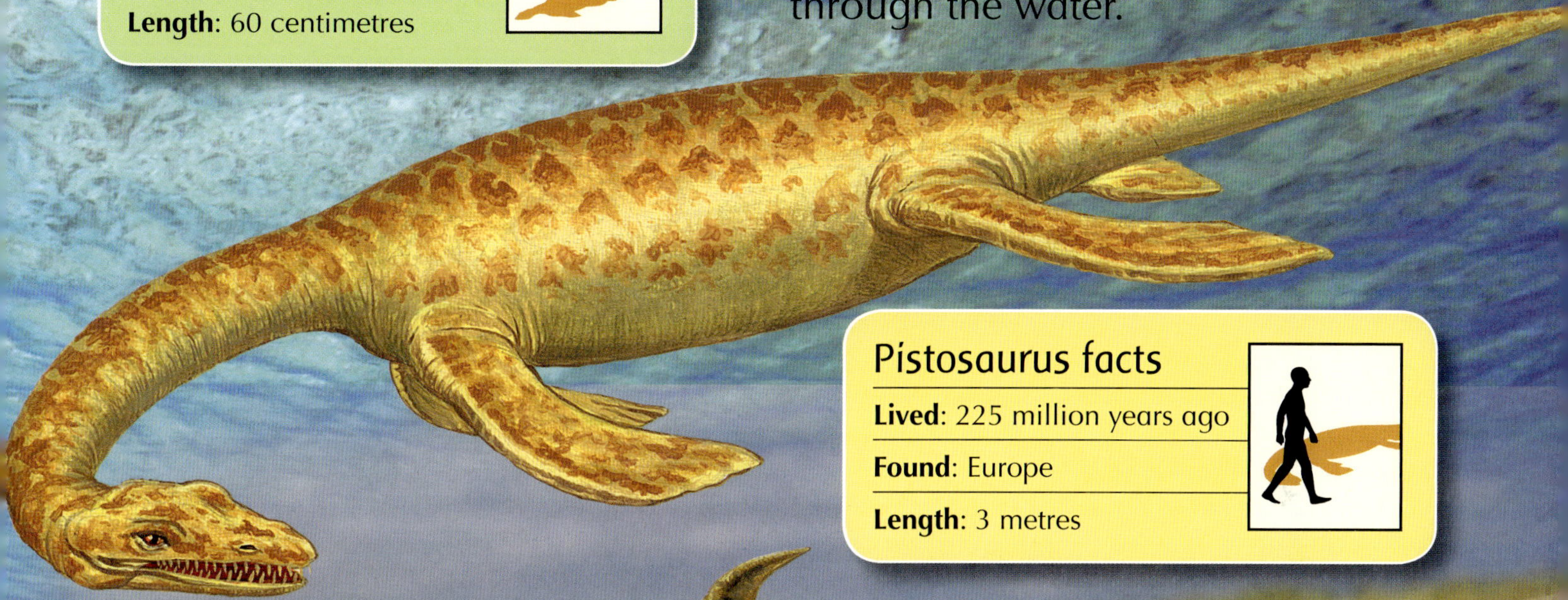

Pistosaurus facts

Lived: 225 million years ago

Found: Europe

Length: 3 metres

Nothosaurus

Like other nothosaurs, this reptile had lots of big, sharp teeth. They fitted together to make a spiky cage for trapping prey such as fish.

Part-time land-lovers

Nothosaurs may have spent time lying on rocks in the sun, just like seals and sea lions do today.

Nothosaurus facts

Lived: 225 million years ago

Found: Asia, Europe, N. Africa

Length: 3 metres

Plesiosaurs

These sea-living reptiles first lived about 200 million years ago. They had small heads and long necks. They fed mostly on fish and other small sea creatures.

Plesiosaurus

This was one of the first plesiosaurs. Like other plesiosaurs, it probably 'flew' through the water by flapping its long flippers up and down, like turtles do today.

Plesiosaurus facts

Lived: 200 million years ago

Found: Europe

Length: 2.5 metres

Cryptoclidus facts

Lived: 150 million years ago

Found: Europe

Length: 4 metres

Cryptoclidus

Cryptoclidus had many smaller joints in its flippers. This gave the flipper a smoother and more flexible curved surface.

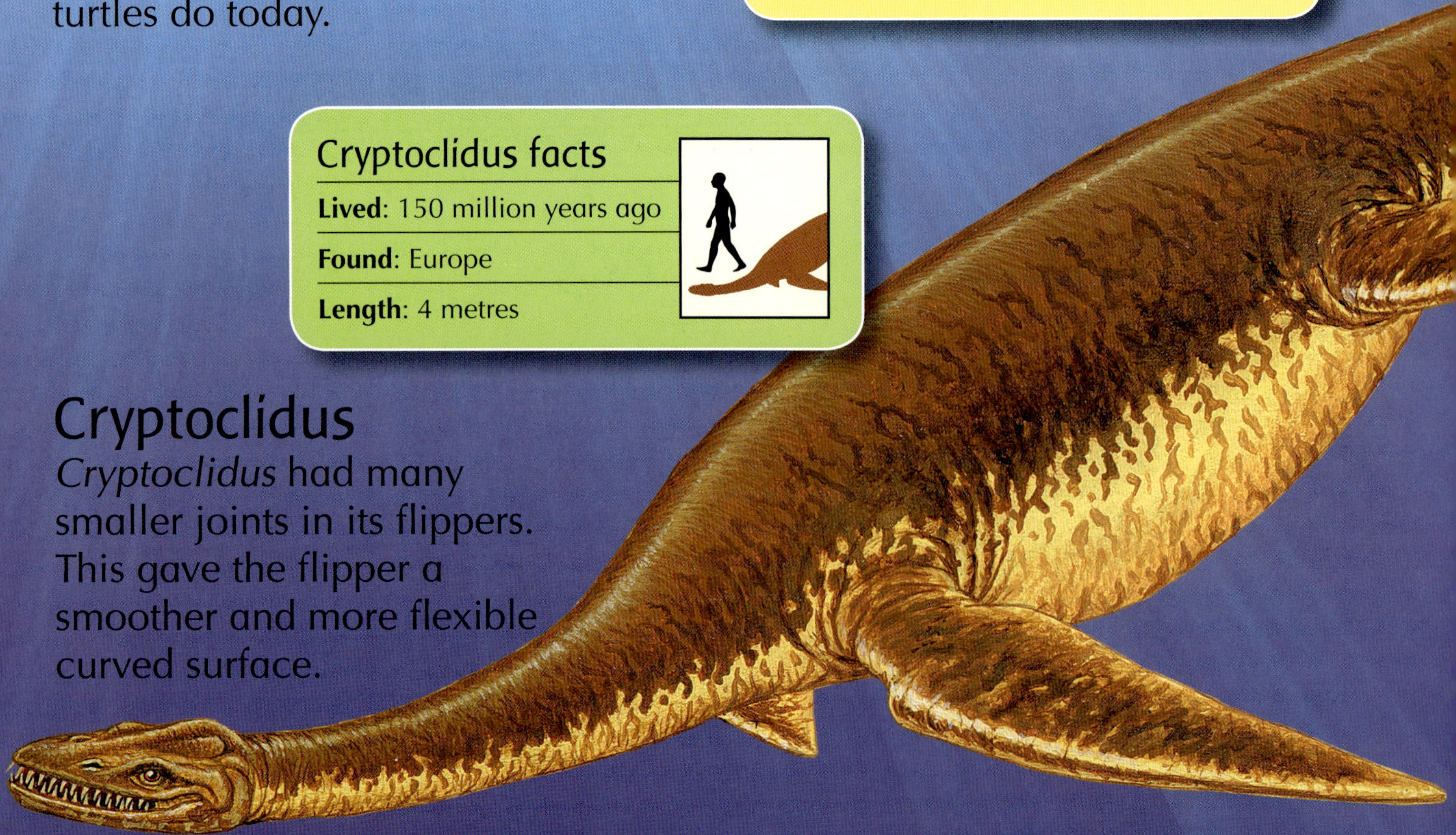

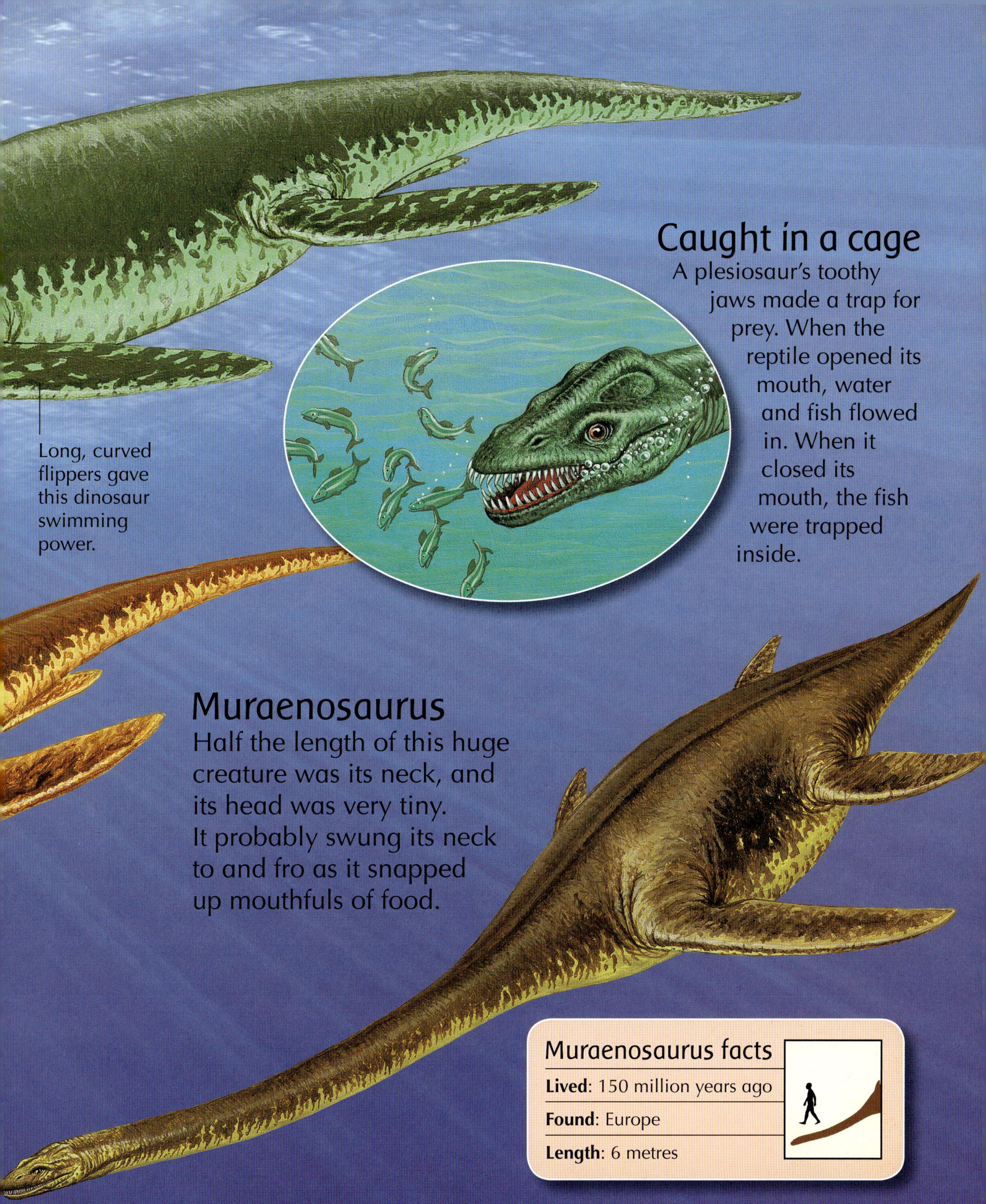

Long, curved flippers gave this dinosaur swimming power.

Caught in a cage

A plesiosaur's toothy jaws made a trap for prey. When the reptile opened its mouth, water and fish flowed in. When it closed its mouth, the fish were trapped inside.

Muraenosaurus

Half the length of this huge creature was its neck, and its head was very tiny. It probably swung its neck to and fro as it snapped up mouthfuls of food.

Muraenosaurus facts

Lived: 150 million years ago

Found: Europe

Length: 6 metres

Dinosaur fact

Elasmosaurus facts

Lived: 70 million years ago

Found: Asia, North America

Length: 14 metres

Half of the *Elasmosaurus's* length was made up of its neck.

Elasmosaurus was the longest of the plesiosaurs.

More bones

Most reptiles have between five and ten vertebrae in their neck. But *Elasmosaurus* had more than 70, making its long neck very bendy.

Skull

Elasmosaurus had a long, low head. Its pointed nose helped it cut through the water and its long teeth made a perfect trap for fishy prey.

Elasmosaurus

Elasmosaurus held its long neck straight out in front of its body.

Fast predator

Elasmosaurus probably ate small prey such as fish, squid and ammonites. It could move its long neck very swiftly to reach and catch its prey.

Eyes on top

Elasmosaurus' eyes were on top of its head. It could see fish swimming above it and reach up to catch them.

Pliosaurs

These reptiles were close relatives of the plesiosaurs. They had short necks and large heads and they were very fierce hunters.

Macroplata facts	
Lived: 200 million years ago	
Found: Europe	
Length: 5 metres	

Taking a breath

A pliosaur's nostrils were on the top of its head. This meant it could easily poke its head above the surface to breathe.

Macroplata

This early pliosaur had quite a long neck, like a plesiosaur. But unlike plesiosaurs, its rear flippers were larger than the front ones.

Peloneustes

Peloneustes had strong cone-shaped teeth. Its jaws were strong so it could bite and hold on to prey such as large fish and squid and even plesiosaurs.

Peloneustes facts

Lived: 145 million years ago

Found: Asia, Europe

Length: 3 metres

Macroplata had a large, long head with rows of teeth like a crocodile.

Kronosaurus facts

Lived: 140 million years ago

Found: Australia

Length: 9 metres

Kronosaurus

This pliosaur was a fierce hunter. It had a huge head that measured 2.7 metres long and lots of big, sharp teeth. It could move quickly by flapping its long flippers.

Liopleurodon

This huge reptile hunted anything that moved. It preyed on other large reptiles such as ichthyosaurs and plesiosaurs.

Dinosaur fact

Liopleurodon facts

Lived: 150 million years ago

Found: Europe, S. America

Length: 25 metres

An ichthyosaur tries to escape *Liopleurodon's* massive jaws.

Liopleurodon was bigger than any of the meat-eating dinosaurs that lived on land.

Good sense of smell

Liopleurodon could smell the different scents of its prey in the water. If the smell was stronger in one nostril than in the other, it would follow that trail.

Skeleton, skull and teeth

Liopleurodon's skull was up to 5 metres long, longer than the whole body of many other dinosaurs. It had teeth like sharp daggers.

Massive!

Liopleurodon was up to 25 metres long and could have weighed over 75 tonnes or even over 150 tonnes. It might have been bigger than the largest animal on the Earth today - the blue whale.

Water support

One reason that *Liopleurodon* could grow so big is that it lived in the sea. This meant that its great weight was supported by the water.

Rise of the ichthyosaurs

The ichthyosaurs, unlike plesiosaurs and pliosaurs, could not move on land. They lived their whole lives in water.

Ichthyosaur skeleton

The skeleton shows that an ichthyosaur was a reptile, not a fish. It had arm and leg bones in its flippers and bones in its tail. Fish do not.

Shonisaurus

Huge *Shonisaurus* had a rounded body and four paddle-like flippers. All four were about the same size.

Ophthalmosaurus

The long, beak-like jaws of this ichthyosaur were more than 1 metre long and ideal for seizing fast swimming prey.

Ophthalmosaurus facts

Lived: 150 million years ago

Found: Europe, North and South America

Length: 4.5 metres

Shonisaurus facts

Lived: 210 million years ago

Found: North America

Length: 15 metres

Shonisaurus had a longer body than a *Tyrannosaurus*.

Mixosaurus

Fossils of this early ichthyosaur have been found in many parts of the world. It had fleshy flaps on the top and bottom of its tail.

Mixosaurus facts

Lived: 220 million years ago

Found: Asia, Europe, N. America

Length: 1 metre

Dinosaur fact

Ichthyosaurus facts

Lived: 200 million years ago

Found: Europe, N. America

Length: 1.8 metres

Some almost-complete ichthyosaur skeleton fossils have been found.

Fossil food

Ichthyosaurus ate fish, squid and curly-shelled ammonites. Fossils of all these creatures have been found with ichthyosaur remains.

Super senses

Ichthyosaurus's ears helped it sense ripples in the water, made by moving prey.

Ichthyosaurus

Lots of fossils of this reptile have been found, so it is one of the best known of all prehistoric animals. This species lived for more than 60 million years.

Ichthyosaurus could crack an ammonite's hard shell with its strong jaws.

Big eyes for hunting

Skeletons show that *Ichthyosaurs* had very big eyes. The largest found were 10 centimetres across.

How deep?

We don't know how deep *Ichthyosaurus* could dive. Relatives of the type of squid it ate live in very deep seas today, down to 1,000 metres.

Turtles and placodonts

The first turtles probably lived on land, like tortoises. But some started to live in the water and developed flippers instead of legs.

Protostega

This turtle had a beak-like mouth but no teeth. It could crush shellfish and jellyfish in its strong jaws.

Protostega facts

Lived: 70 million years ago

Found: North America

Length: 3 metres

Holes in the shell

The shell of some turtles was not solid but made of pieces of bone covered with thick, rubbery skin. This made the shell lighter, so the turtle could move quickly.

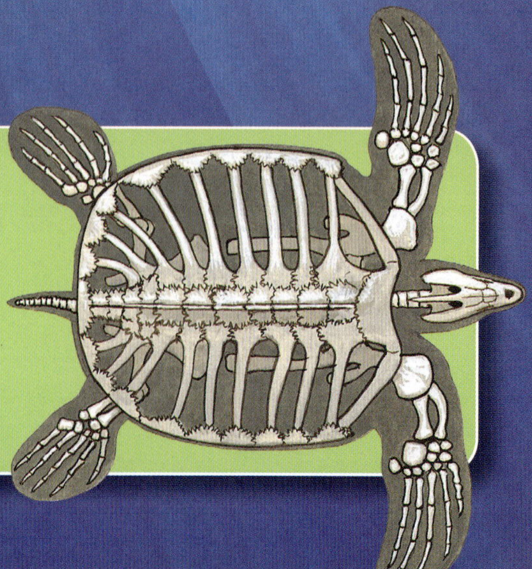

Placochelys facts

Lived: 210 million years ago

Found: Europe

Length: 90 centimetres

Placochelys

Placochelys looked like a turtle but it belonged to another group of reptiles called placodonts. They lived at the same time as nothosaurs.

Eggs on beaches

The first turtles laid their eggs on land, just like turtles today. They came out onto the beach and laid their eggs in holes in the sand.

Henodus

This reptile was also a placodont. Its square-shaped shell protected it from predators such as sharks.

Henodus facts

Lived: 210 million years ago

Found: Europe

Length: 1 metre

Sharks

These sea-living predators were around before the dinosaurs and are still the most feared hunters in the sea today. Sharks are fish, not reptiles.

Cretoxyrhina

Cretoxyrhina was a top predator in the late Cretaceous seas. It would have attacked pliosaurs, crocodiles and even mosasaurs.

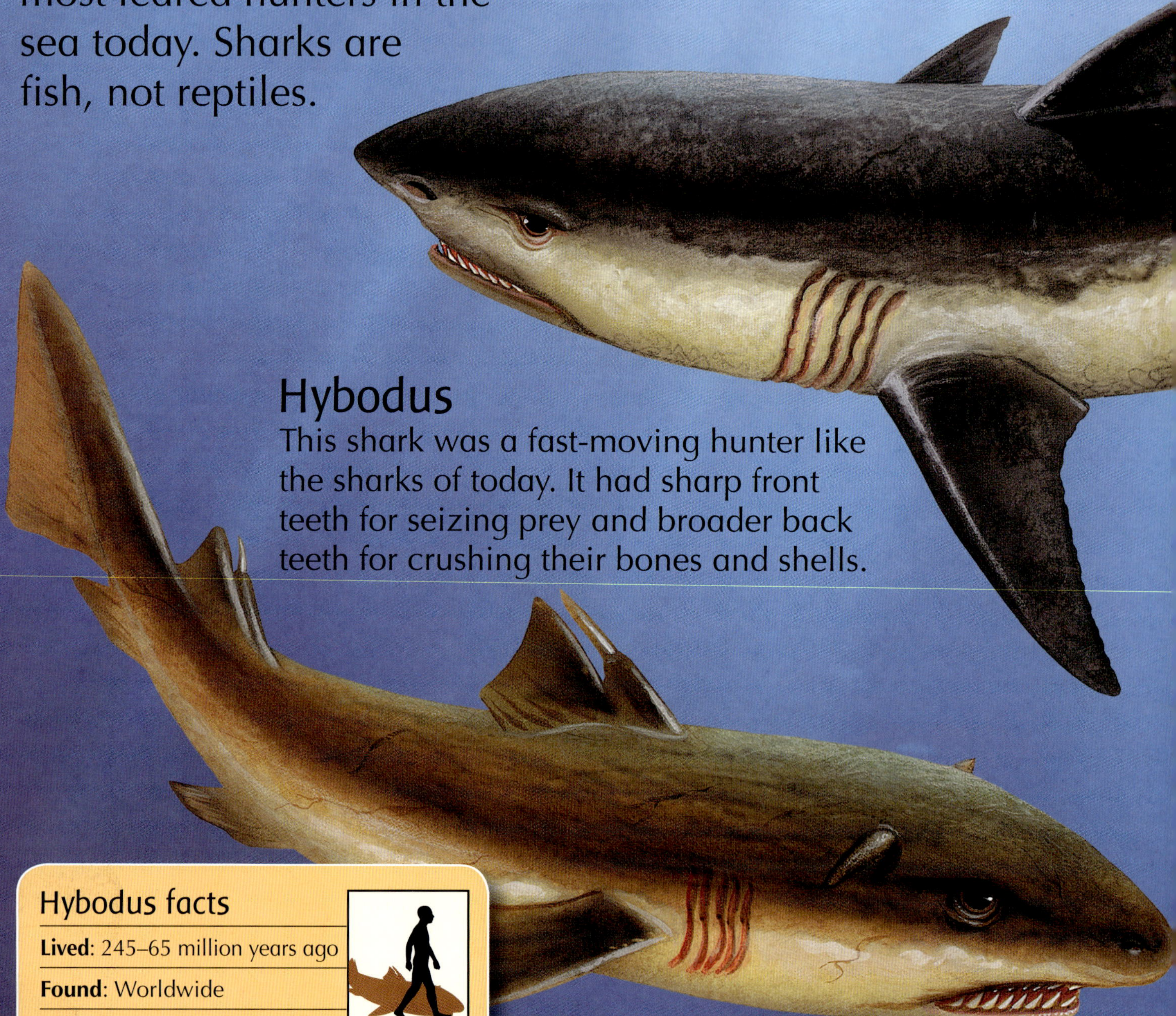

Hybodus

This shark was a fast-moving hunter like the sharks of today. It had sharp front teeth for seizing prey and broader back teeth for crushing their bones and shells.

Hybodus facts

Lived: 245–65 million years ago

Found: Worldwide

Length: 2 metres

Cretoxyrhina facts

Lived: 70 million years ago

Found: North America

Length: 5.4 metres

Its sleek shape made this fish a fast swimmer.

DID YOU KNOW?

A shark's skeleton is made mainly of cartilage (gristle), not from bone.

Teeth

The teeth of ancient sharks were very much like those of sharks today. They were very sharp with jagged edges, like a triangular steak knife, for cutting into their prey.

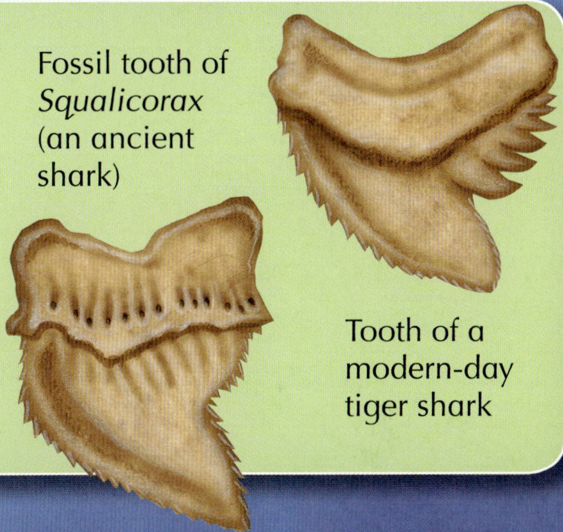

Fossil tooth of *Squalicorax* (an ancient shark)

Tooth of a modern-day tiger shark

Scapanorhynchus

This shark's jaws opened very wide so it could take big bites of its prey. No one knows why it had such a long, pointed nose.

Scapanorhynchus facts

Lived: 100 million years ago

Found: Worldwide

Length: 50 centimetres

Mosasaurs

These reptiles were huge, sea-living lizards. They lived at the same time as the dinosaurs and died out 65 million years ago.

Globidens

This mosasaur had different teeth from its relatives. They were about the same size and shape as golf balls and just right for crushing shellfish such as crabs.

Tylosaurus facts

Lived: 70 million years ago

Found: North America

Length: 9 metres

Tylosaurus

Like most mosasaurs, *Tylosaurus* had four paddle-like flippers and a huge mouth with lots of sharp teeth. It had a long tail edged with flaps top and bottom.

Clidastes

Clidastes was small for a mosasaur but still as big as most sharks today. It may have hunted near the shore, leaving the giant mosasaurs to the open ocean.

Clidastes facts

Lived: 70 million years ago

Found: North America

Length: 3.5 metres

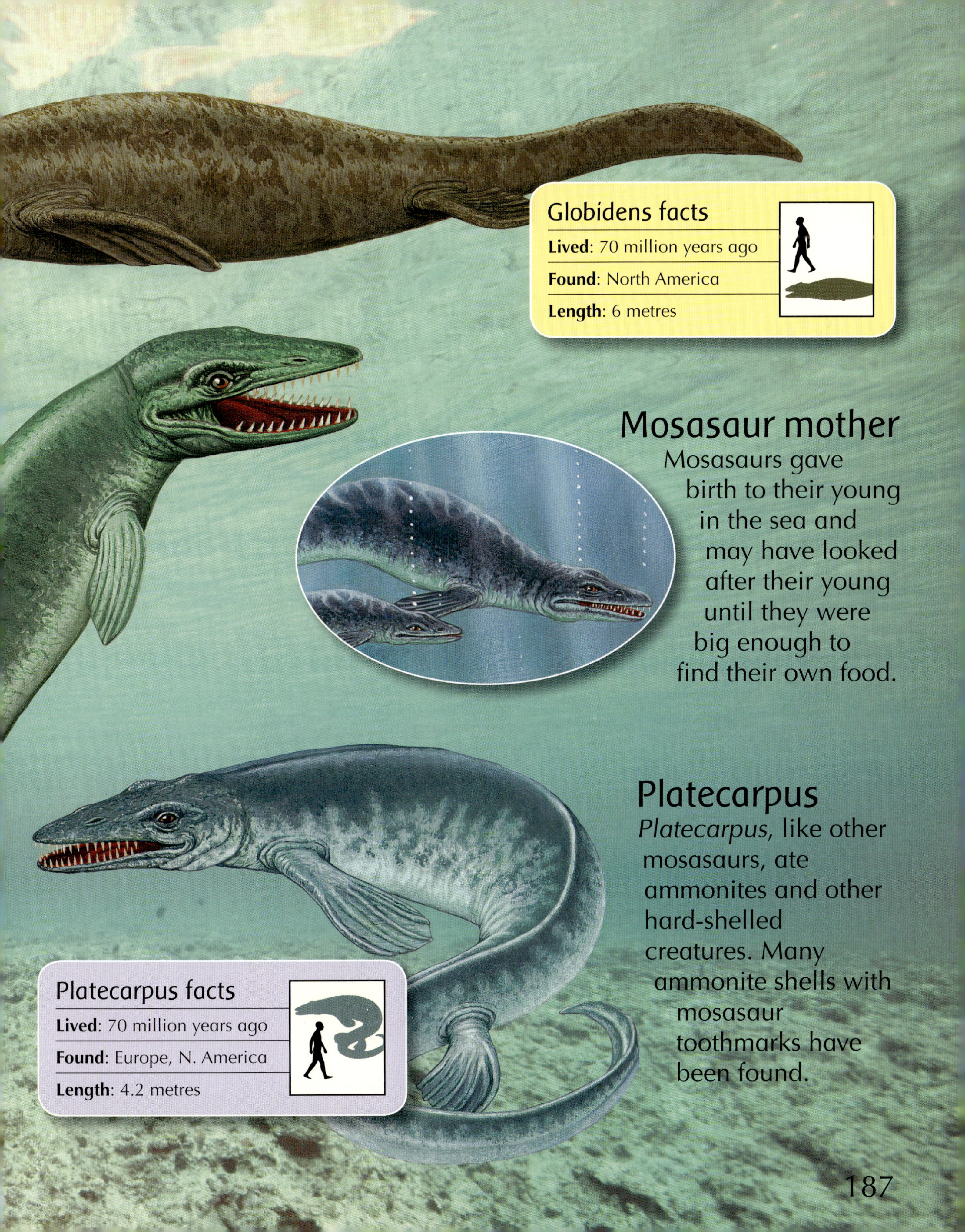

Globidens facts
Lived: 70 million years ago
Found: North America
Length: 6 metres

Mosasaur mother

Mosasaurs gave birth to their young in the sea and may have looked after their young until they were big enough to find their own food.

Platecarpus

Platecarpus, like other mosasaurs, ate ammonites and other hard-shelled creatures. Many ammonite shells with mosasaur toothmarks have been found.

Platecarpus facts
Lived: 70 million years ago
Found: Europe, N. America
Length: 4.2 metres

Mosasaurus

Mosasaurs are named after an area in the Netherlands called the Meuse. Huge fossil jaws and teeth from a mosasaur were dug up there in the 1770s.

Dinosaur fact

Mosasaurus facts

Lived: 70 million years ago
Found: Europe, N. America
Length: 10 metres

When mosasaurs died out, sharks took over the seas.

The name *Mosasaurus* means 'Meuse lizards'. It had a long streamlined body.

Mosasaur skeleton

The skeleton of a mosasaur shows that it had arm and leg bones like a lizard's. It also had a powerful bendy lower jaw, just as monitor lizards of today do.

Swimming tail

This reptile's flippers were small and weak. It probably swam by moving its long body and tail from side to side like a huge snake.

Hunting

This huge creature was a fierce hunter, even more powerful than the biggest sharks today. It could catch almost anything in the sea, even giant turtles.

Origins

The ancestors of mosasaurs were probably big meat-eating lizards. These lizards began living in the sea and their legs gradually became paddle-like flippers.

The world of the dinosaurs

No human being has ever seen a living, breathing dinosaur. But we still know a lot about these creatures that lived millions of years ago. Scientists can study fossilized bones and teeth. They compare them with those of living animals to figure out how dinosaurs looked and how they lived.

History of the Earth

There were creatures living on the land 150 million years before the dinosaurs and the first tiny life forms lived in the ocean more than 2,000 million years ago.

Eras and periods

The Earth's history is divided into lengths of time called eras. The dinosaurs lived in the Mesozoic era. Each era is split into smaller lengths of time called periods.

Cenozoic era *(Recent life)*	Quaternary period	Holocene epoch (0.01–Now)	*Most of recorded history*
		Pleistocene epoch (2–0.01)	*Early humans spread*
		Tertiary period (65–2)	*Rise of mammals and birds*
Mesozoic era *(Middle life)*		Cretaceous period (144–65)	*Last of the dinosaurs*
		Jurassic period (206–144)	*Dinosaurs reach their greatest size*
		Triassic period (250–206)	*Many reptiles, first dinosaurs*
Paleozoic era *(Ancient life)*		Permian period (286–250)	*Mammal-like reptiles*
		Carboniferous period (360–286)	*Many amphibians, first reptiles*
		Devonian period (408–360)	*First amphibians walk on land*
		Silurian period (438–408)	*Plants spread from water to land*

All numbers are millions of years ago

How time is divided

The eras and periods are worked out according to the way the rocks of the time formed, and the fossils in those rocks.

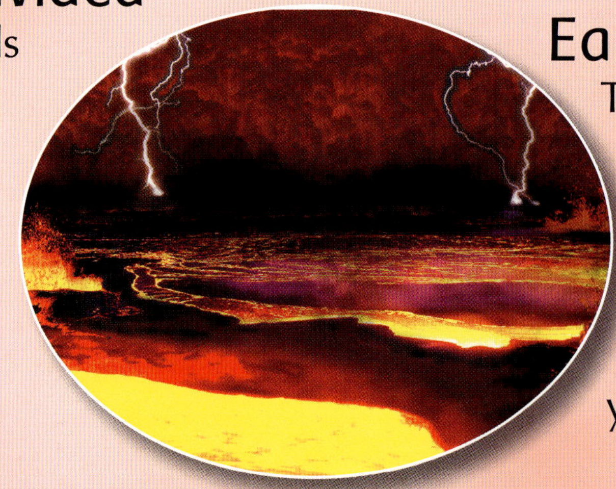

Early Earth

The Earth was formed about 4,600 million years ago. At first nothing could live on Earth, but life began about 3,000 million years ago.

Moving continents

The worlds land has slowly moved and split into the continents we know today.

In the Triassic all the land was in one mass known as Pangaea.

The Triassic period

The earliest dinosaur fossils have been found in rocks dating from the middle of the Triassic period, about 230 million years ago.

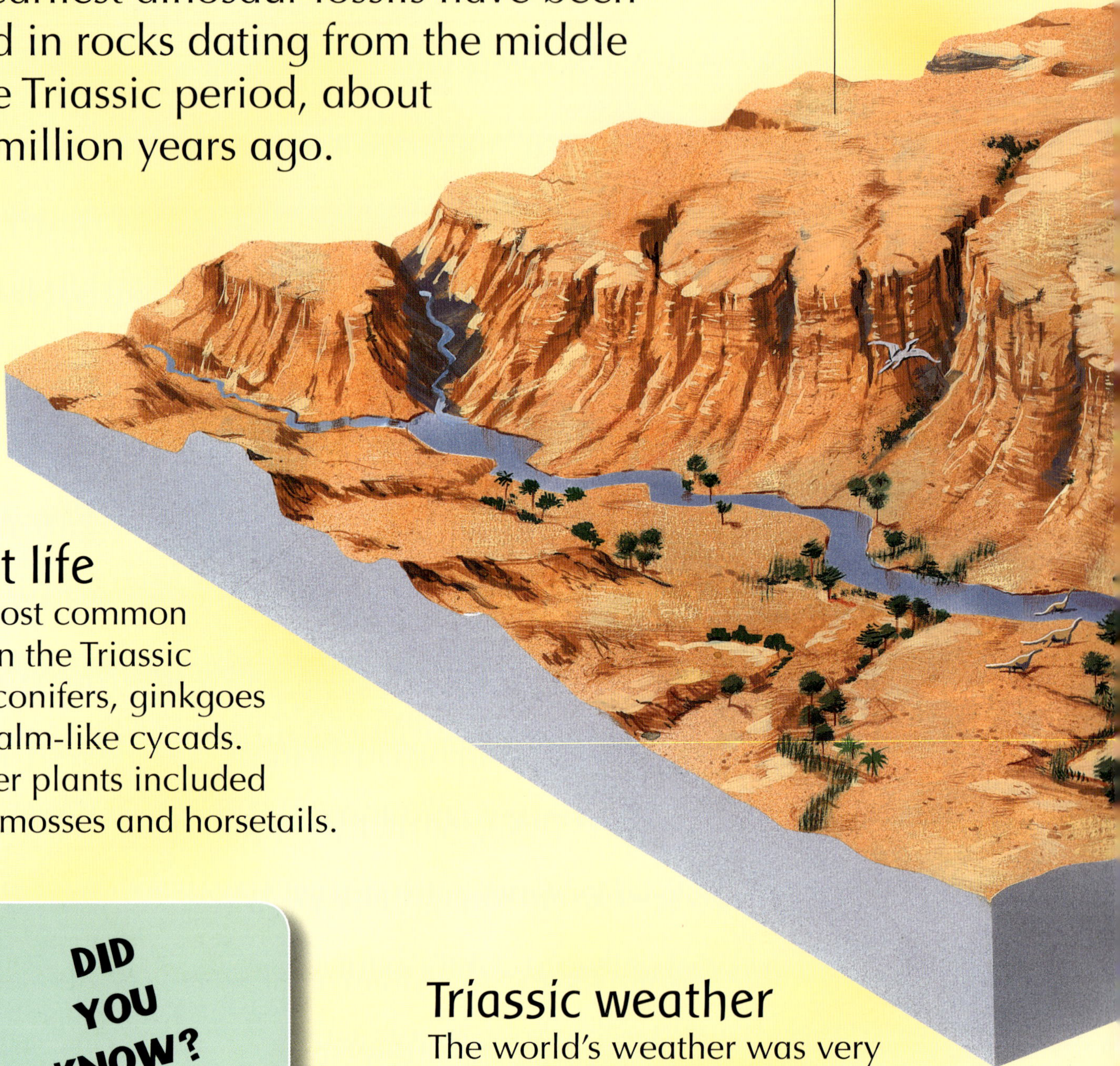

There were huge deserts in the centre of the land.

Plant life

The most common trees in the Triassic were conifers, ginkgoes and palm-like cycads. Smaller plants included ferns, mosses and horsetails.

DID YOU KNOW?

The world was so warm during the Triassic that there was no ice at the North and South Poles.

Triassic weather

The world's weather was very different in the Triassic. It was much warmer than it is now and there was less rain. This meant there were large areas of desert and dry scrubland.

Triassic map

At this time there was just one big land mass we call Pangaea. All around it was the Panthalassa Ocean. But the Tethys Sea was beginning to divide Pangaea in two.

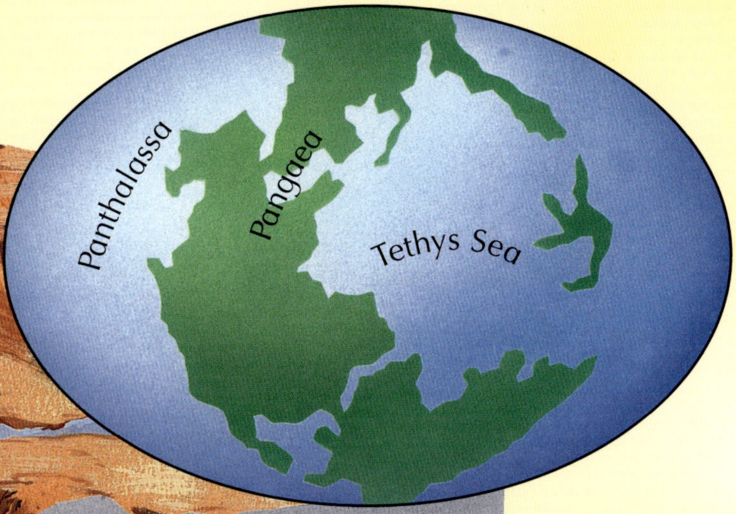

Triassic animals

There were many kinds of reptiles as well as dinosaurs in the Triassic. These included mammal-like reptiles, crocodiles and turtles. The first mammals had also appeared.

The Jurassic period

At the start of the Jurassic period, about 200 million years ago, the world began to change again. The climate became cooler and more plants grew.

Plant life

Plants began to grow in areas which had been deserts. The main trees were still conifers. Smaller plants included clubmosses, ferns and horsetails.

DID YOU KNOW?

The world's continents are still moving, but only at the rate of a few centimetres a year.

Jurassic weather

The weather was warmer than today, but not as hot as it was during the Triassic. The climate was much the same all over the world with long rainy seasons and short dry seasons.

Jurassic map

Pangaea separated into two large areas of land. These were Gondwanaland in the south and Laurasia in the north.

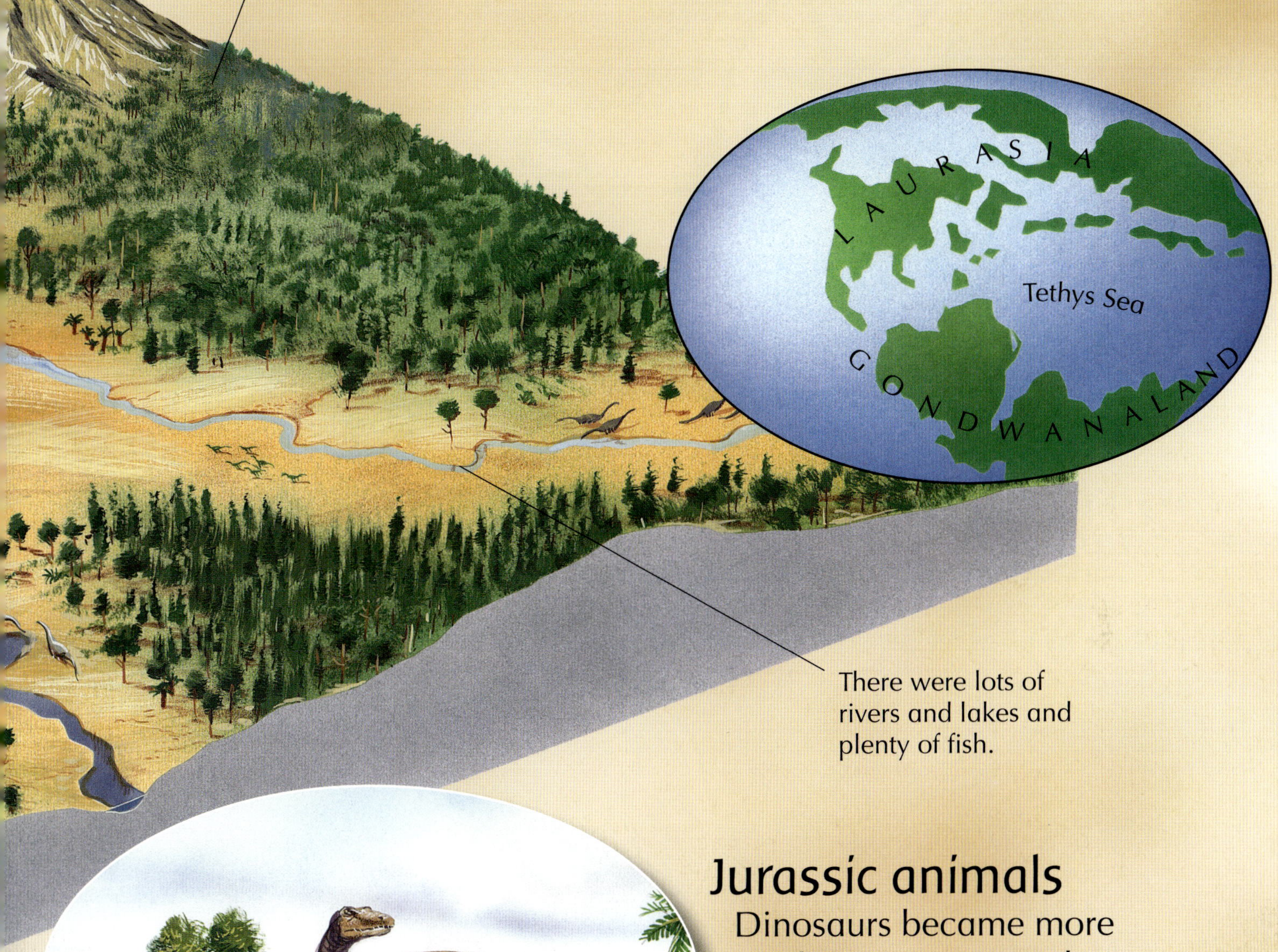

Jurassic animals

Dinosaurs became more and more common during the Jurassic and there were lots of smaller reptiles too, such as lizards. There were insects, snails and spiders and the first birds appeared.

The Cretaceous period

During the Cretaceous period the world became more like it is today. It started to be much colder at the poles and hotter near the Equator.

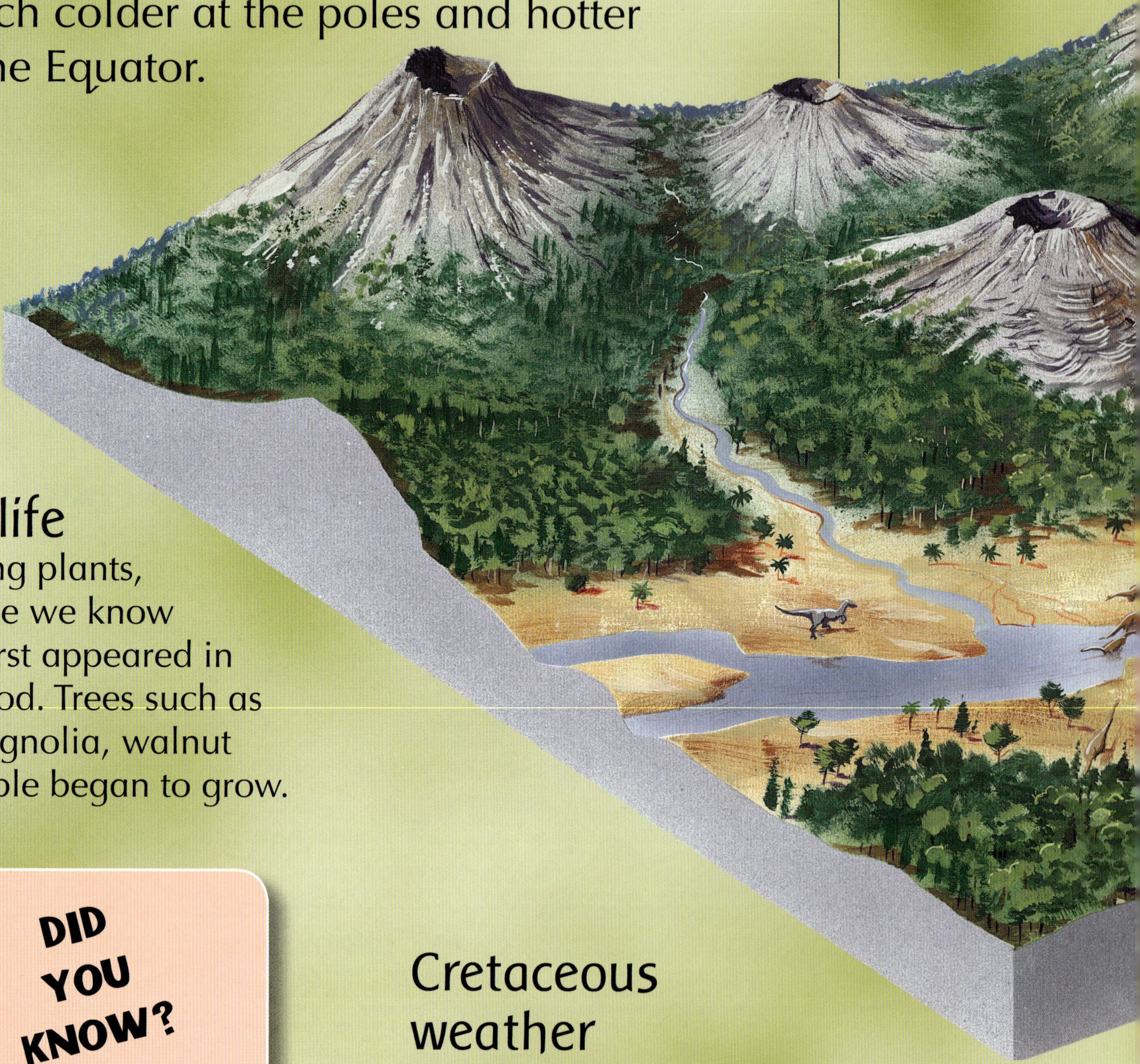

Moving continents caused many mountains to appear.

Plant life

Flowering plants, like those we know today, first appeared in this period. Trees such as oak, magnolia, walnut and maple began to grow.

DID YOU KNOW?

At least 1,000 different kinds of dinosaur have been discovered and there may be many more.

Cretaceous weather

The seasons became more varied at this time. In the north and south there were winters and summers. Nearer the Equator there were wet and dry seasons.

Cretaceous map

Laurasia and Gondwanaland broke up into the continents we know today. The Americas drifted away from Europe and Africa so the Atlantic Ocean became wider.

Cretaceous animals

There were more kinds of dinosaur than ever, as well as other reptiles such as snakes. Birds flew in the skies along with flying reptiles called pterosaurs. There were some small mammals.

Dinosaur skeletons

Most of what we know about dinosaurs comes from studying their fossilized bones and teeth.

Dinosaur posture

A dinosaur's legs were held straight down under its body. (The legs of reptiles such as lizards stick out to the sides of the body.)

Hip bones

Dinosaurs can be divided into two groups depending on the shape of their hip bones.

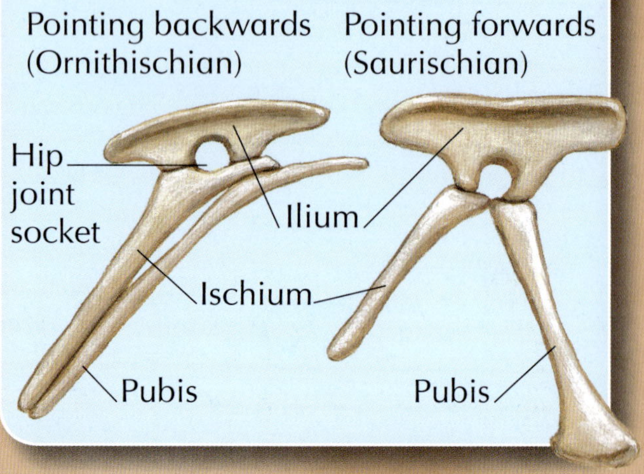

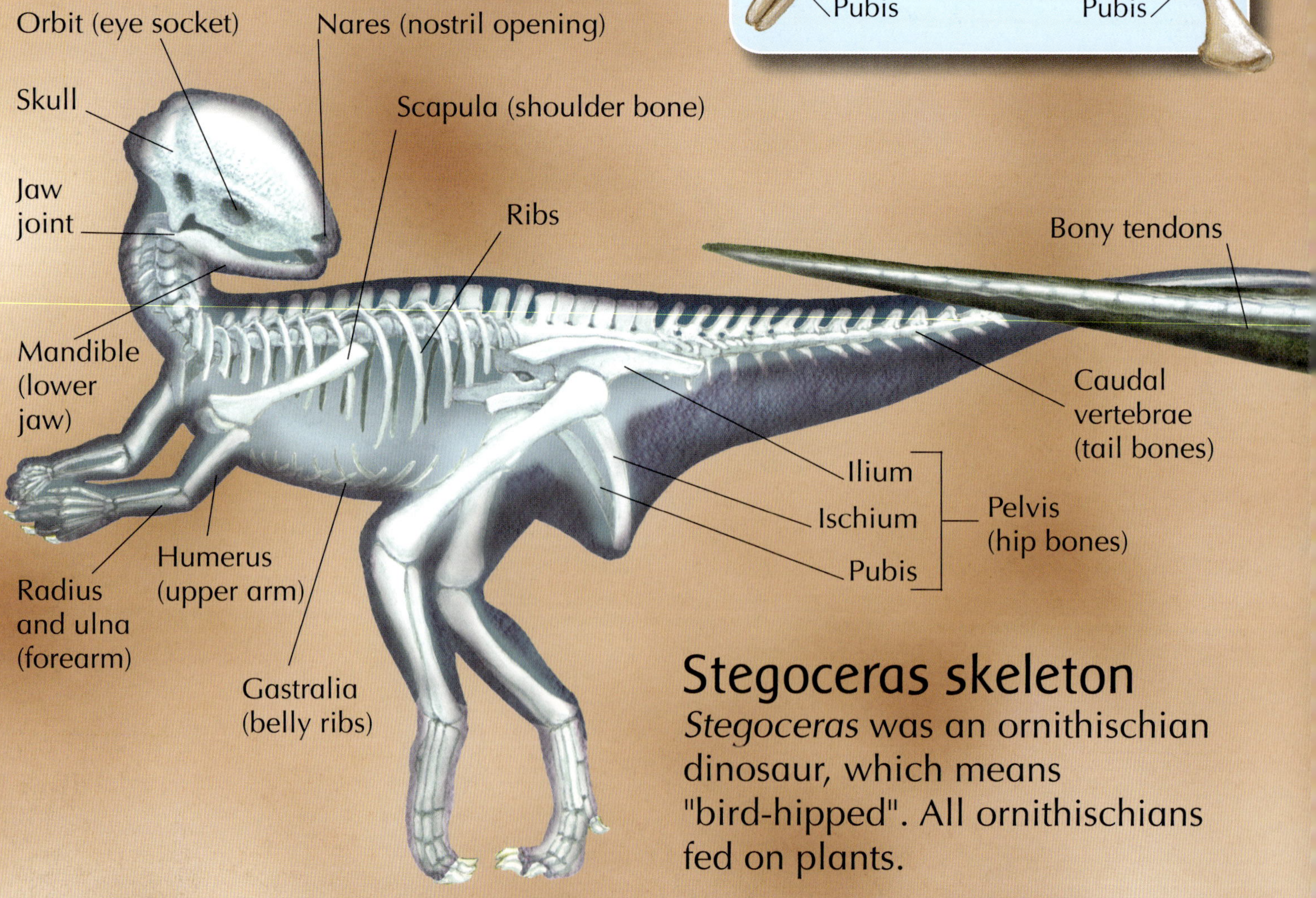

Stegoceras skeleton

Stegoceras was an ornithischian dinosaur, which means "bird-hipped". All ornithischians fed on plants.

Joint types

A tendon is the end of a muscle where it joins the bone. Some dinosaurs had stiff bony tendons on their tail joints, making the tail extra strong and very rigid.

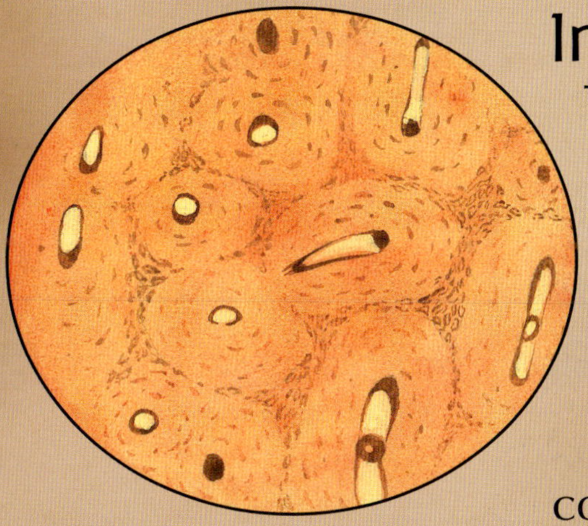

Inside fossil bone

The bones of some fast-running dinosaurs like *Deinonychus* show that they may have been warm-blooded like mammals, not cold-blooded like most reptiles.

DID YOU KNOW?

More dinosaur fossils have been found in North America and Asia than anywhere else.

Deinonychus skeleton

Deinonychus was a saurischian dinosaur, which means 'lizard-hipped'. There were meat-eaters and plant-eaters in this group of dinosaurs.

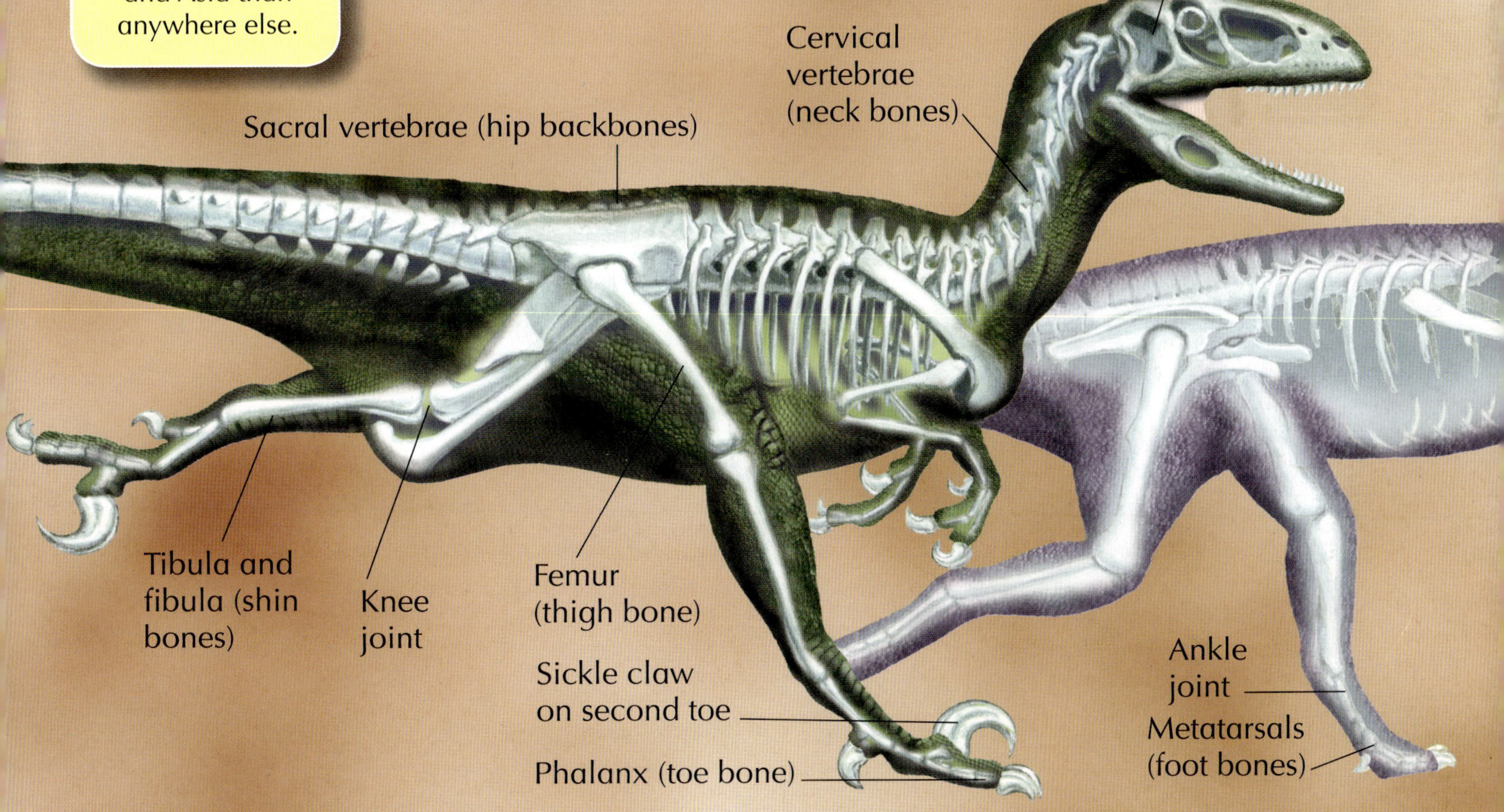

Dinosaur muscles and organs

Experts can work out what dinosaur muscles and organs may have looked like by studying similar living animals.

Brains

Models of a dinosaur's brain can be made using the shape of the space inside the skull.

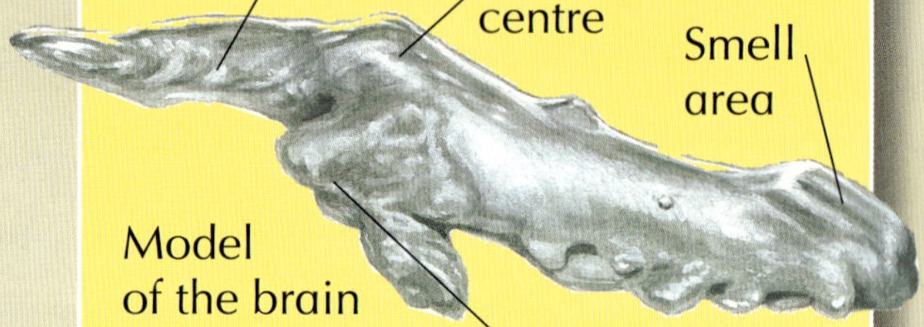

Digestive system

The big plant-eating dinosaurs swallowed their food whole. It was broken down inside the part of the body called the gizzard.

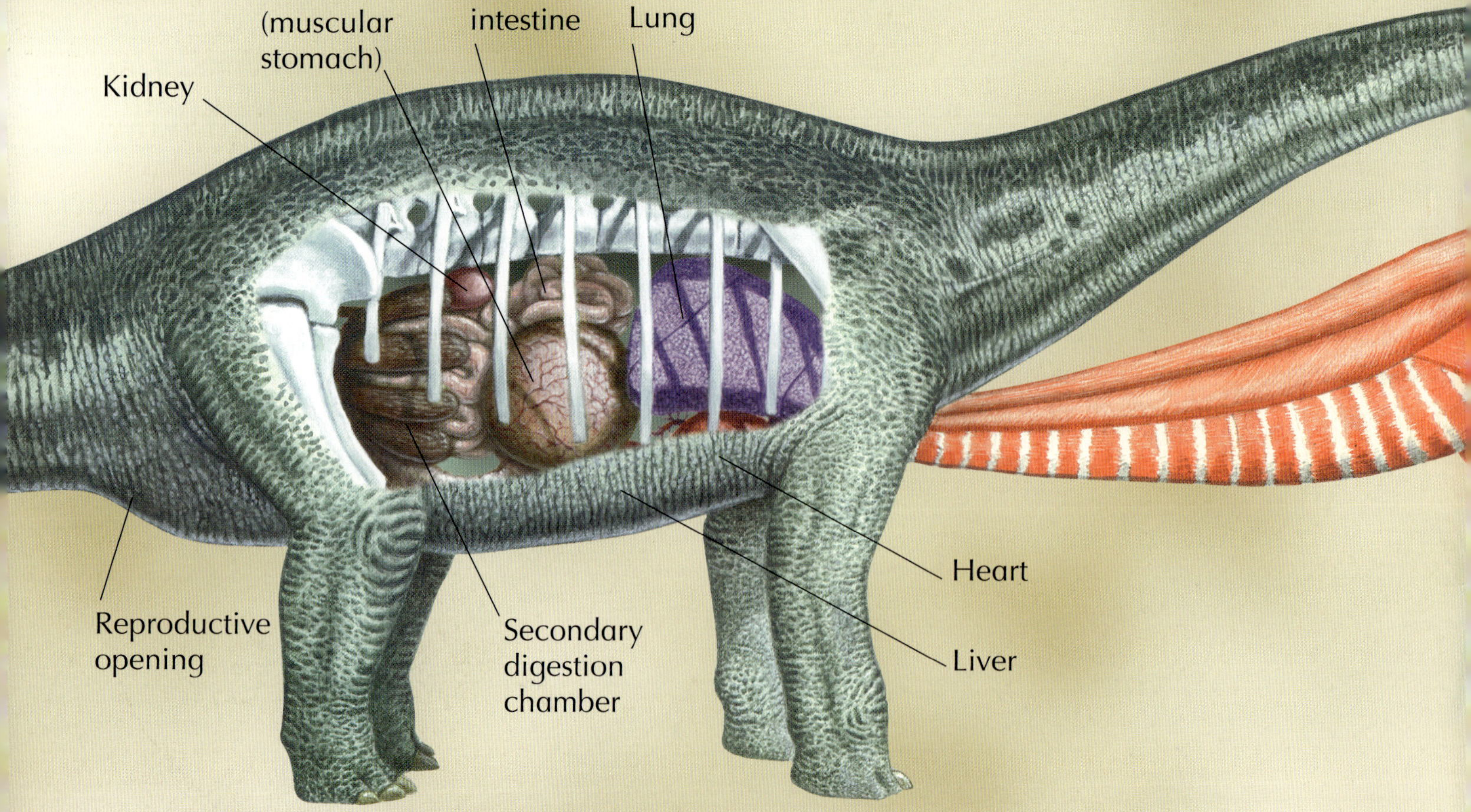

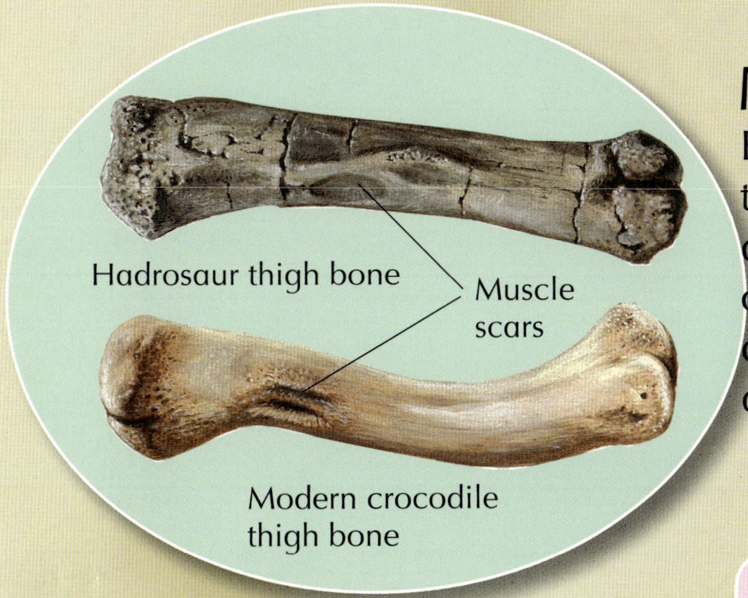

Muscle scars

Experts check to see whether the marks of muscles on fossil dinosaur bones look like those on the bones of similar living animals. This helps them learn about the dinosaur.

DID YOU KNOW?

The first fossils of dinosaur footprints were found in the USA in 1802 by a young boy on a farm.

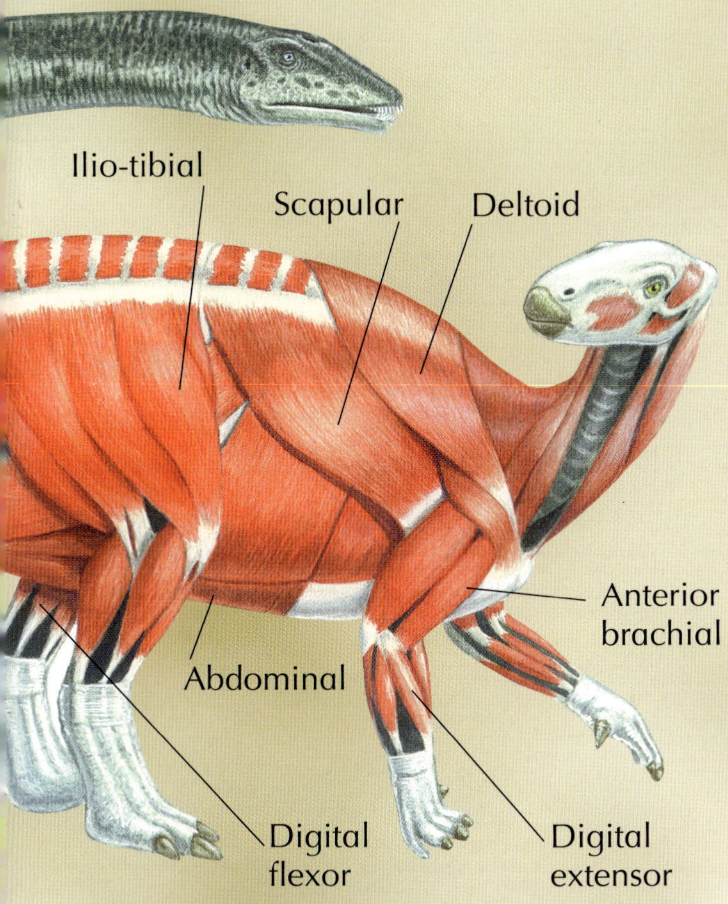

Clues to muscles

Marks on bones show where muscles were attached in life. This helps experts work out how big the muscles might have been and how the animal moved.

Naming the muscles

Many muscles are named after their shape, such as the deltoid – deltoid means triangular. Others are named after the bones they are attached to such as the femoro-tibial (thigh-shin).

Death of the dinosaurs 1

From time to time lots of living things die out. About 65 million years ago, dinosaurs and many other creatures disappeared.

Not only dinosaurs

Flying reptiles called pterosaurs in the air, and mosasaurs and plesiosaurs in the sea also became extinct around 65 million years ago.

How long?

Dinosaurs were wiped out 65 million years ago. But this did not happen instantly. By 70 million years ago there were already fewer dinosaurs than before.

The asteroid impact

An asteroid is a piece of rock from space. Some people think that an asteroid hit Earth 65 million years ago.

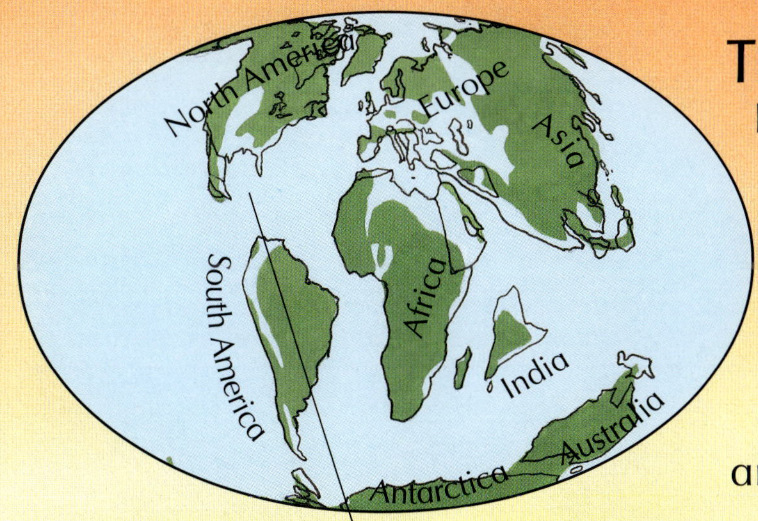

An enormous crater found off the coast of Mexico may be the asteroid's impact site.

The asteroid idea

If an asteroid did hit the Earth 65 million years ago it would have caused huge clouds of dust and debris to spread. This would have blocked out the sun for years so plants died. Without plants, plant-eating animals died too, and then meat-eating animals.

DID YOU KNOW?

The asteroid of 65 million years ago might have measured 10 kilometres across and travelled at 55 kilometres per second.

Dinosaur fact

There has been lots of research into what caused the dinosaurs to die out but there is still no confirmed reason.

Perhaps dinosaurs and other animals were killed by a deadly disease that spread across the world.

Climate change

The movement of the world's land (see page 193) may have caused climate change. If the weather became very cold, dinosaurs might have frozen to death.

Invisible rays

If a huge star had exploded in space, the radiation could have reached Earth.

Death of the dinosaurs 2

There are lots of other ideas about why the dinosaurs died out. A few are unlikely – for example, some people think that aliens came down and killed them!

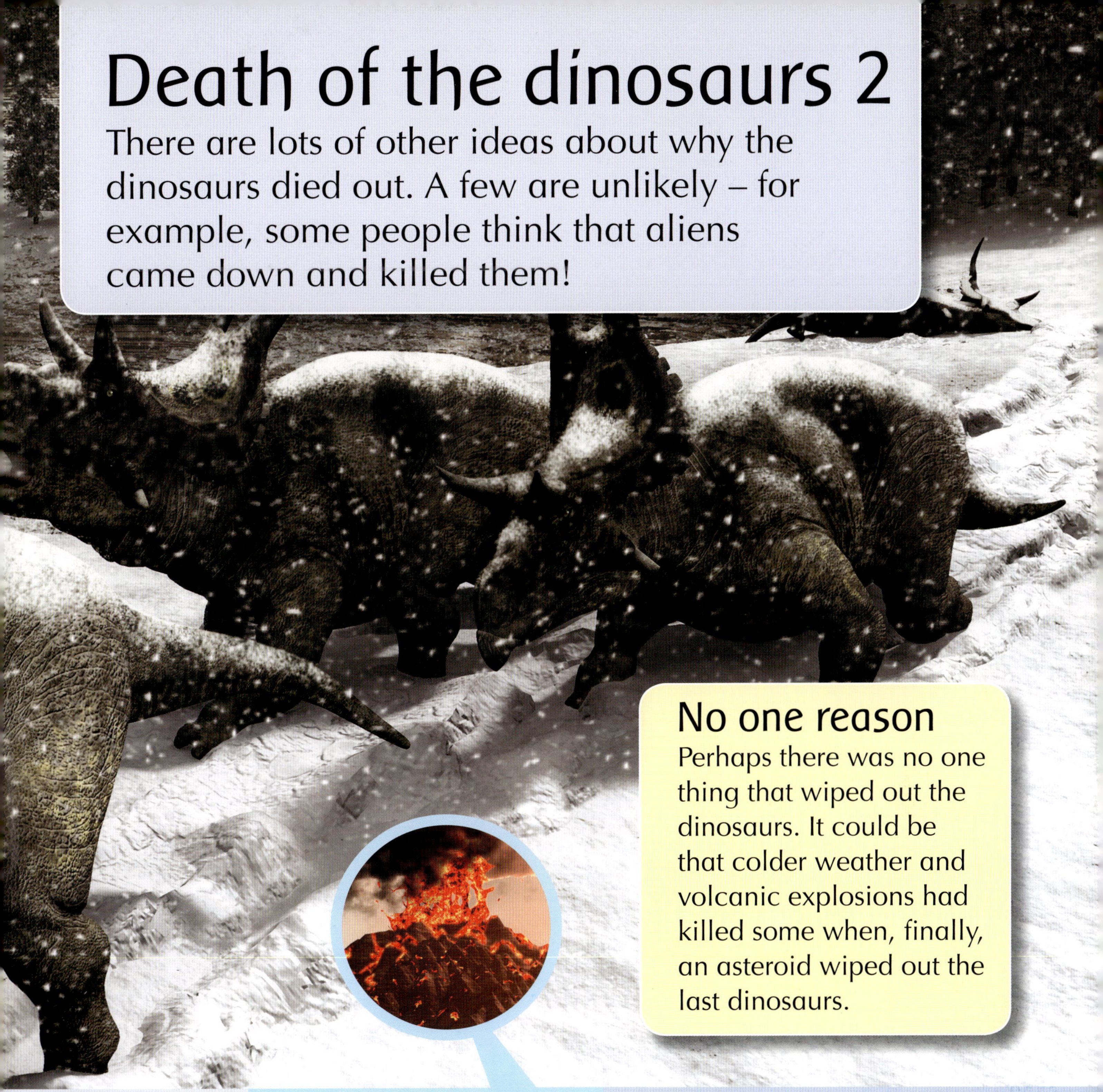

No one reason

Perhaps there was no one thing that wiped out the dinosaurs. It could be that colder weather and volcanic explosions had killed some when, finally, an asteroid wiped out the last dinosaurs.

Choked to death

Lots of volcanoes were erupting 65 million years ago. The air might have been full of poisonous smoke and dust that killed many plants and animals.

This would have killed large animals such as dinosaurs. They could not hide underground as mammals could.

The survivors

These ideas may explain why some animals were wiped out, but not why others lived. For example, if dinosaurs were killed by a disease, why did shellfish and some plants disappear too?

After the dinosaurs

Once the dinosaurs had disappeared, mammals began to take over. They ruled life on land, just as the dinosaurs had done before them.

An early start

Mammals had lived alongside the dinosaurs. But they were small and shrew-like. None were bigger than a pet cat today.

Taking over

Mammals began to change and many different types evolved. Grasses first grew 25 million years ago and grass-eating mammals developed to feed on them.

The last takeover

Humans began to evolve about 4 million years ago, in Africa. One type of ape began to walk upright on two legs, and another type began to use tools.

Not all survived

There were lots of kinds of mammals in the Tertiary period, from huge many-horned rhinos to small, early horses. There were many reptiles too, just as there are today.

Dinosaurs all around?

Some experts believe that birds are a type of dinosaur. This would mean that dinosaurs are not extinct at all but flying all around us.

How fossils are formed

Fossils are the remains, traces or impressions of dead animals or plants. These became trapped in the ground and turned into rock over thousands of years.

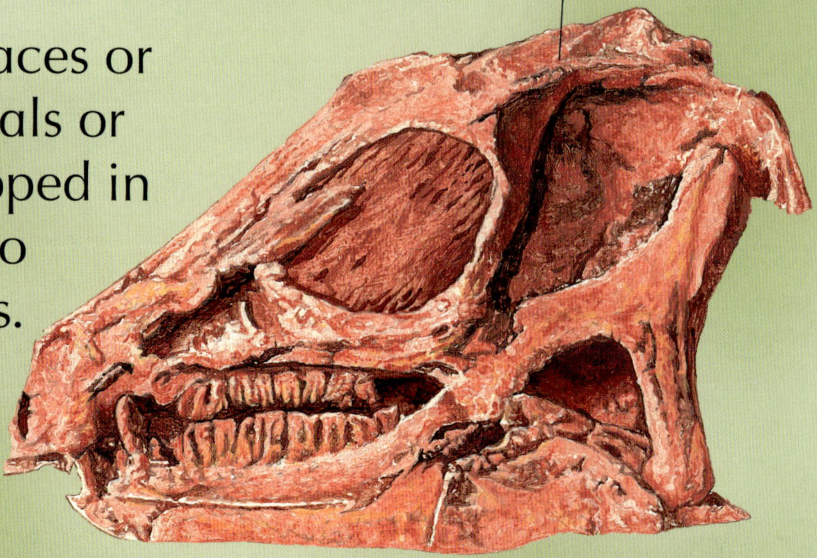

What forms fossils?

Only the hard parts of an animal can be fossilized. So there are fossil bones, teeth, claws and shells. There are many fossils of shelled sea creatures such as ammonites.

Teeth and bone fossils

As the tooth or bone lies in the ground, substances called minerals gradually sink into it. The tooth or bone stays the same shape but slowly turns to rock.

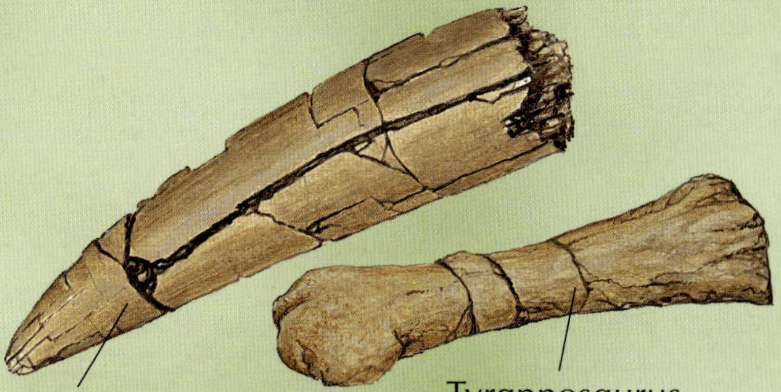

DID YOU KNOW?

The oldest fossils of animals that have ever been found date from about 600 million years ago.

Bone to stone

The dead bodies of most animals rot away. Very few become fossils. The picture opposite shows what happens over millions of years if the conditions are just right.

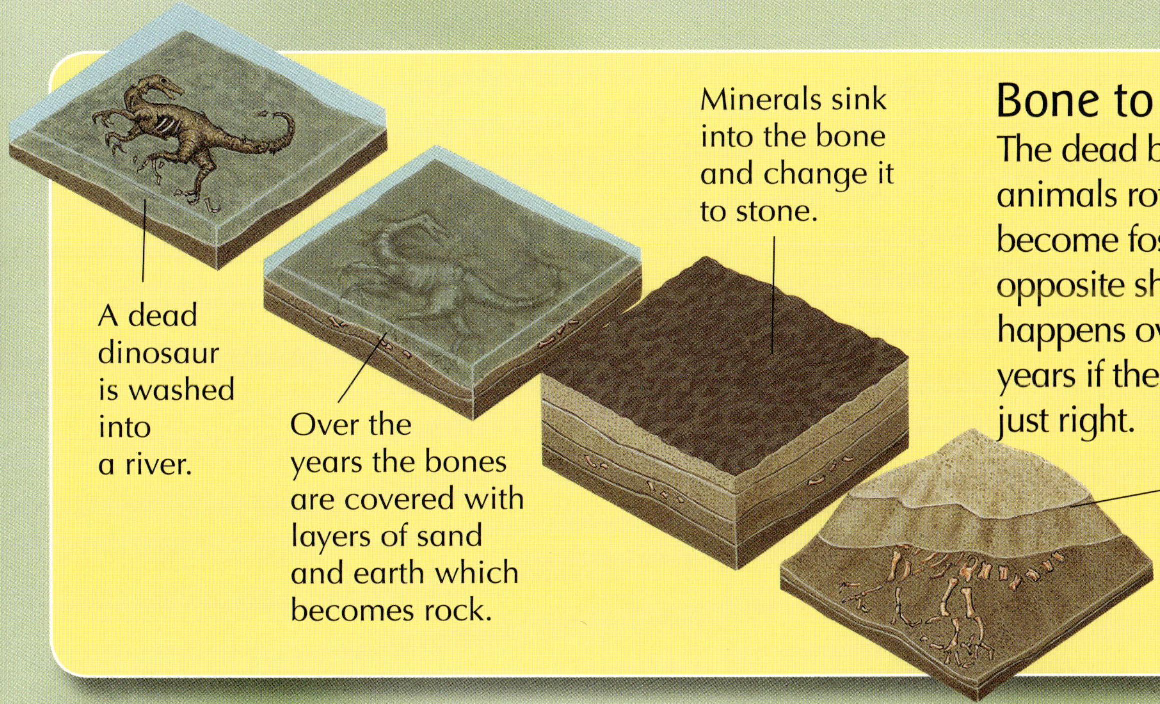

Trace fossils

The shape of a footprint or a nest can also be turned to stone. This is called a trace fossil. Even droppings (coprolites) and eggshells can be fossilized.

True fossils

A true fossil is a fossil of a body part such as bone or tooth. Some fossils of dinosaur skin have been found but these are very rare.

Perfectly preserved

Amber is sticky fluid called resin that oozes from a tree trunk. Some ancient pieces have been found with the remains of an insect trapped inside.

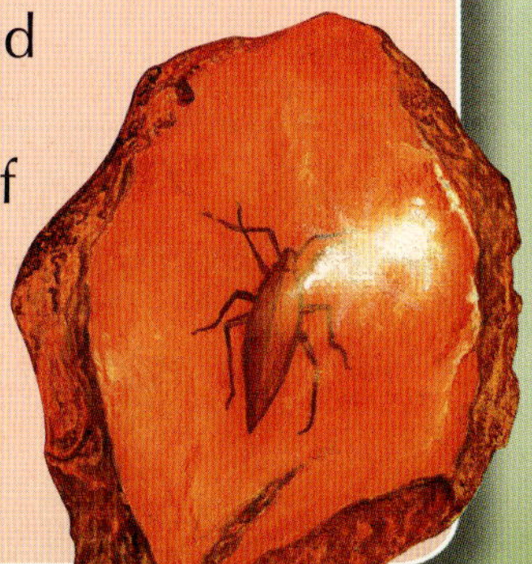

Digging for dinosaurs

Fossils are hard to find, but in some places, rocks from the age of the dinosaurs have been worn away by wind and weather so fossils are nearer the surface.

Searching for sites

Digging for fossils is hard work. Experts look for clues, such as a bone or tooth sticking out of a cliff or rock, to see if a dig may be worthwhile.

Every find is carefully labelled.

Tools and techniques

Explosives may be used to uncover fossils. Then lots of tools such as hammers and chisels are used to break away the rock around the fossil.

The finds continue...

Dinosaur experts like Paul Sereno are still finding new kinds of dinosaurs. Who knows what amazing creatures are still to be discovered?

Diggers must take great care not to damage fossils.

DID YOU KNOW?

Dinosaur fossils have now been found in every continent of the world, even in Antarctica.

Displaying dinosaurs

You can see dinosaur fossils in museums in many countries of the world. Some museums also have lifelike models which move and even roar!

Cleaning

Tiny hand tools and brushes are used to take away every bit of dirt from a dinosaur fossil. The cleaning process can take weeks or even months.

Life-size dinosaurs are an amazing sight.

Preparing and sorting

Rebuilding a dinosaur from pieces of fossil is like putting together a very difficult jigsaw. Experts use their knowledge of similar creatures to put the pieces together.

The right pose

Dinosaur experts do their best to display dinosaurs as they think they would have looked when they were alive.

Copied bits

It is very rare to find a whole dinosaur skeleton so some parts have to be made to fill in the gaps. Sometimes the fossils are copied in light material such as fibreglass.

On display

At last, when everything has been put together and missing pieces filled in, the dinosaur goes on display. We can all admire a creature that lived so many millions of years ago.

Seeing inside rocks and fossils

Medical scanners are used to see inside fossils. They show what condition the fossil is in and whether it is worth cleaning and preparing.

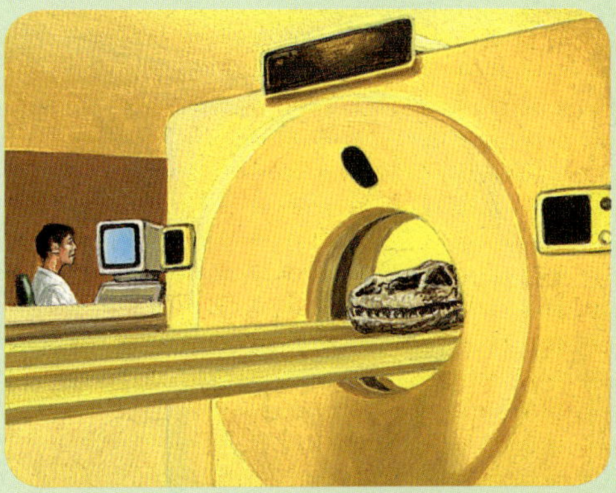

Some useful words and Index

In this section you will find explanations of some of the words dinosaur experts use, and an index of all the dinosaurs and other prehistoric creatures included in this book.

Some useful words

Amphibian

An animal with a backbone and four legs that lays its eggs in water, such as a frog. In the larval (young) stage it lives in water. In the adult stage it lives on land and in water.

Anapsid

A reptile whose skull does not have an opening behind the eye, such as a turtle.

Ankylosaur

An armoured dinosaur covered with bony plates, knobs and spines.

Biped

An animal that stands, walks, or runs on its two hind legs. Humans are bipeds.

Carnivore

An animal that eats meat.

Ceratopsian

A large plant-eating dinosaur with pointed horns and a bony frill growing from the back of its skull.

Cheek teeth

Teeth located behind the front teeth or beak that are used for chewing, especially by plant-eaters.

Cold-blooded

A term used to describe an animal that receives most, or all, of its body heat from external sources, usually the sun.

Conifer
A tree or shrub that produces seed cones, such as fir and pine trees.

Coprolites
Fossilized animal droppings.

Cycad
A non-flowering plant with a thick trunk, no branches, and palm-like leaves. Cycads are related to today's conifers.

Dental battery
A large number of interlocking teeth that form a tough grinding surface.

Diapsid
A reptile whose skull has two openings on either side, such as a lizard.

Dinosaur
A reptile with an upright posture, not a sprawling one like a lizard.

Embryo
The early stages in the development of a plant or an animal.

Evolution
The process by which a plant or animal changes over time.

Extinction
The disappearance of a species of animals or plants.

Family
A group of animals or plants which are related to each other.

Fern
A non-flowering plant with finely divided leaves called fronds.

Fossil
The remains of a dead animal or plant. Dinosaur fossils could be bones and teeth, footprints, coprolites, gastroliths, eggs, or skin impressions.

Gastrolith
Stone found in the stomachs of some plant-eating dinosaurs to help them break down and digest vegetation.

Ginkgo
A tree that looks like a conifer but which sheds its leaves in the autumn. The only living species of ginkgo is the maidenhair tree.

Gondwanaland
The ancient southern super-continent, made up of today's Africa, Australia, Antarctica, South America and India.

Hadrosaur
A large plant-eating dinosaur with a wide, flat beak. Also called a duck-billed dinosaur.

Herbivore
An animal that only eats plants.

Horsetail
A plant with an upright stem and tiny leaves. Horsetails are related to ferns.

Ichthyosaur
A dolphin-like reptile that lived in the sea.

Iguanodont
A plant-eating dinosaur with hoof-like nails on its hind feet and spikes instead of instead of thumbs on its hands.

Invertebrate
An animal without a backbone.

Laurasia
The ancient northern super-continent, made up of today's North America, Europe and Asia.

Mammal
A warm-blooded animal covered with hair, which feeds its young with milk.

Omnivore
An animal that eats both meat and plants.

Order
A group of animals or plants that belong to related families. There are two orders of dinosaurs – Ornithischia and Saurischia.

Ornithischia
One of the two orders of dinosaurs. It includes bird-hipped, plant-eating dinosaurs such as the ankylosaurs, ceratopsians and stegosaurs.

Ornithomimid
A fast-running, meat-eating dinosaur with a long neck and slender legs, similar in appearance to a present-day ostrich.

Ornithopod
A two-legged plant-eater. Some ornithopods had crests on their heads.

Pachycephalosaur
A two-legged plant-eater with a thick skull.

Pangaea
The single land mass or super-continent of the Permian period. It broke up during the Triassic period. The name means all Earth.

Plesiosaur
A long-necked reptile that lived in the sea.

Predator
An animal that kills other animals (prey) for food.

Prey
The animal that is killed by a predator.

Quadruped
An animal that stands, walks, or runs on all four limbs.

Reptile
A cold-blooded animal with scales and a backbone that lays its eggs on land.

Saurischia
One of the two orders of dinosaurs. Saurischia are lizard-hipped dinosaurs, including the theropods and sauropods.

Sauropod
A bulky, long-necked, long-tailed plant-eater that walked on all four feet.

Scute
A bony plate set into the skin of a dinosaur.

Serrated
Notched along an edge, like the teeth of theropods.

Stegosaur
A large plant-eating dinosaur with rows of triangular bony plates on its back and spines on its tail.

Synapsid
A mammal-like reptile whose skull has one opening on either side.

Thecodont
A big, heavy reptile that crawled on all four legs. Thecodonts were probably the ancestors of dinosaurs.

Theropod
A two-legged meat-eating dinosaur, such as *Allosaurus* and *Tyrannosaurus*.

Vertebra
A bone of the backbone. The plural is vertebrae.

Vertebrate
An animal with a backbone.

Warm-blooded
A term used to describe an animal that can control its own body temperature, such as a mammal or a bird.

Index

Q

R

S

T

U

V

W